ANDY MCI.

Seeing the Bride in All the Scriptures

First published by Hayes Press 2020

Copyright © 2020 by Andy McIlree

All rights reserved. No part of this publication may be reproduced, stored or transmitted in any form or by any means, electronic, mechanical, photocopying, recording, scanning, or otherwise without written permission from the publisher. It is illegal to copy this book, post it to a website, or distribute it by any other means without permission.

Andy McIlree asserts the moral right to be identified as the author of this work.

Unless otherwise attributed, all poetry is written by Andy McIlree.

Unless otherwise stated, all Scripture references are taken from the New King James Version (NKJV). Copyright © 1982 by Thomas Nelson, Inc. Used by permission. All rights reserved.

Scriptures marked NIV are from THE HOLY BIBLE, NEW INTERNATIONAL VERSION® NIV® Copyright © 1973, 1978, 1984, 2011 by International Bible Society®. Used by permission. All rights reserved worldwide.

Scriptures marked ESV are from The Holy Bible, English Standard Version® (ESV®) Copyright © 2001 by Crossway, a publishing ministry of Good News Publishers. All rights reserved.

Scriptures marked NASB are taken from the NEW AMERICAN STANDARD BIBLE®, Copyright © 1960,1962,1963,1968,1971,1972,1973,1975,1977,1995 by The Lockman Foundation. Used by permission.

Scriptures marked KJV are from the HOLY BIBLE, King James Version, Public Domain 1611.

Scriptures marked RV are from the HOLY BIBLE. Revised Version, Public Domain 1881/1885.

First edition

ISBN: 978-1-78910-209-3

*This book was professionally typeset on Reedsy.
Find out more at reedsy.com*

Contents

Preface	iv
1 THINGS CONCERNING HIMSELF	1
2 EVE: A BRIDE THROUGH BLOOD	8
3 REBEKAH: A BRIDE THROUGH THE SPIRIT	19
4 ISRAEL: A BRIDE FOR GOD	30
5 THE SHULAMITE: A BRIDE FOR THE KING	41
6 RUTH: A BRIDE THROUGH REDEMPTION	53
7 A BRIDAL RESEMBLANCE IN THE CHURCHES	63
8 SEEING THE DIFFERENCES	74
9 SUFFERING OR REJOICING	84
10 A GLORIOUS CHURCH	94
11 THE BRIDE, THE WIFE OF THE LAMB	106
12 FURTHER THOUGHTS ON "FOREVER"	118
13 CONCLUSION: OF HIM AND FOR HIM	131
FOOTNOTES	134
ABOUT THE AUTHOR	139
MORE BOOKS FROM ANDY MCILREE	140
ABOUT THE PUBLISHER	144

Preface

We have already enjoyed looking at those who can be described as 'Men God Moved,' and have seen how men such as Peter, Jude and Boaz[1] were stirred and carried along by the Holy Spirit to fulfil God's purpose. Now, we welcome you to think of 'Women God Moved,' and see how He also used them: some, by their godly example; others, because of the imagery conveyed by the place they occupy in His Word.

Along with everything God wants us to gain from this study, Christian women should be assured that He never devalues them. To prove this, He has used a series of Bible brides to occupy very special places in His purpose, and emphasise that He elevates them to the highest possible level by using them as examples of what He calls "the bride, the Lamb's wife."[2] For our first in-depth study together, we have quite a journey ahead of us, so let's go for a walk.

The two who did this in Luke 24 had no idea how their walk would turn out, yet it was the most momentous one they ever took, for "Jesus Himself drew near and went with them."[3] What they didn't anticipate was that He was about to take them on a different kind of walk, one in which only He could be their Travel Guide on a journey through the Old Testament. He even gave them good reason to give His talk a title – "The things concerning Himself"[4] or, as A.M. Hodgkin called it, 'Christ in all the Scriptures.' What He shared, we don't know, but there's no doubt at all that He went through prophecies and events that foreshadowed His life on earth, His sufferings, and entrance to glory. What an unforgettable walk that was!

In a similar way, we can take another walk through the same Old Testament books to trace the reason for His coming and His death on the cross, but, as we set out on this journey, we will also need a very real sense that Jesus is drawing near. Why? Because only the great Expositor Himself, through the present working of the Holy Spirit, can guide us step-by-step on our quest of 'Seeing the bride in all the Scriptures' from the dust of earth in the second chapter of Genesis to the glory of heaven in the second last chapter of the Revelation. As with seeing the Saviour Himself in all the Scriptures, our walk begins in Genesis and continues in the Books of the Law, before flowing on through the Psalms and the Prophets. At the outset, we acknowledge that we have the right to explore the Word, but clear pictures will not emerge unless we give the Lord the right to explain. When He does, the effect on us ought to mirror how the two from Emmaus felt when they asked, "Did not our heart burn within us while He talked with us on the road, and while He opened the Scriptures to us?"[5] May ours be the same!

1

THINGS CONCERNING HIMSELF

The Old Testament is rich in tracing our present theme, and this Introduction anticipates that we will find this to be particularly true in *"the things concerning Himself."* Seeing 'Christ in all the Scriptures' is a profitable study, and the Inspirer has made sure that whatever we consider of Him in the New Testament is amply foreshadowed in the Old and never contradicted.

*Lowliness and loftiness

When Paul wrote about *"the meekness and gentleness of Christ,"*[1] as one well schooled in Old Testament writings he knew that he was in full agreement with the prophets. Speaking of the Saviour's humanity, Isaiah had written *"He shall grow up before Him as a tender plant,"*[2] and Zechariah pinpoints His final entry to Jerusalem with this fitting message, *"Rejoice greatly, O daughter of Zion! Shout, O daughter of Jerusalem! Behold, your King is coming to you, He is just and having salvation, lowly and riding on a donkey, a colt, the foal of a donkey."*[3] No wonder then, that both Matthew and John quote this, and all four Gospel writers include it in their detailed record of the One who said, *"I am gentle and lowly in heart"*[4] and proved it right to the end. Isaiah 53's account is so detailed and accurate that ten times over the New Testament draws from it.

- v.1 - "Lord, who has believed our report" (Jn 12:38; Rom.10:16);
- v.4 - "He himself took our infirmities and bore our sicknesses" (Matt.8:17);
- vv.5,6,9 - "Nor was deceit found in His mouth" (1 Pet.2:21-25);
- v.7 - "He was led as a lamb to the slaughter" (Jn 1:29);
- vv.7,8 - "He was led as a sheep ... His life is taken from the earth" (Acts 8:28-35);
- v.12 - "He was numbered with the transgressors"(Mk.15:28; Lk.22:37).

The end of Isaiah 52, from verse 13 to 15, has been described as an anteroom to chapter 53, and what an entrance it is for it shows that Isaiah *"testified beforehand the sufferings of Christ and the glories that would follow."*[5] Listen to him as he says, *"He shall be exalted and extolled and be very high,"* and then follow the steps of his exaltation of Christ. In his own language, he writes, *"Yārūm wᵉnissā' wᵃgābhah mᵉ'ōdh"*, which combines *rūm* (set on high), *nāsā'* (magnified on high) *gabhāh* (raised up high) and *meōdh* (wholly, utterly). This makes the Hebrew phrase imply high, higher, and highest, so, following His humiliation, this is His threefold exaltation: firstly, in resurrection by rising from the dead; secondly, in His ascension by rising to heaven; and thirdly, in His glorification by rising to the throne to sit *"at the right hand of the Majesty on high."*[6]

Twice in his letter to the Ephesians, Paul describes Him as *"far above all,"*[7] as *"far above all principality and power"* and *"far above all the heavens."* As co-equal within the triune Being, He has gone highest of all, and His Father has said to Him *"Your throne, O God, is forever and ever."*[8] In His incarnation, His lowliness took Him to the lowest depths of death; and in resurrection His loftiness has taken Him to the highest heights of heaven. He is *"Head of the church"* and *"Head over all things to the church."*[9] What a Bridegroom!

*Weakness and mightiness

Among many aspects of His servanthood, Jesus in His manhood subjected Himself to hostility and abuse He could never have known in heaven. Apart from being disgraced and despised, *"He was oppressed and He was afflicted,"*[10] which put Him in the position of being harshly treated, as if by taskmasters and exactors. Again, He allowed it to happen, knowing that the real reason for His coming would prove that *"the weakness of God is stronger than men."*[11] Anger and murder are as old as Genesis 4, and the weakness of Cain was strong enough to kill his brother, but not to raise him from the dead. Calvary would prove that those who, like Cain, were *"of the wicked one"*[12] would deny and slay *"the Holy and Just."*[13] They saw how frail He became as *"He was crucified in weakness,"* but never expected that death to be overcome by resurrection as He rose *"by the power of God."*[14] Only He had that power. They couldn't do it, and they had no power to undo it!

Being identified with weakness was part of His lowliness and humanity; being identified with power and might is part of His loftiness and Deity. But in what way was He weak? In His nature? No, for there could be no weakening of His resolve, His willingness, or His character. By the power of His spoken word some *"went backward, and fell to the ground"*[15] in Gethsemane, and we can only imagine what could have happened had He spoken to Pilate and to Roman soldiers in the same way at Gabbatha and Golgotha. It must only have been by restrained power that they were not similarly affected. As for His weakness, it belonged to His body as the torture of crucifixion brought emaciation to it. In coming to earth to die, He felt sorrow, suffering, pain, and thirst, but His resurrection confirmed, *"Death no longer has dominion over Him."*[16] The purpose of His coming meant that, in His weakness, death mastered Him; but rising showed that, in His mightiness, He mastered death – for Himself, and for His church. Death was the only way for the Sacrifice to provide atonement for believing sinners, and the only way Home for the Saviour. Through His death, He triumphed over His weakness, and by the same means our weakness also has been overcome.

*Sinfulness and sinlessness

The great marvel of the Gospel is this, *"He was despised and rejected of men"*[17] that we might be *"loved"* and *"accepted"*[18] by Him. God allowed them to do their worst to Him, so that He could give His best to us. But there was much more. God did what men couldn't do: He made His own Son to be sin *"for us."* This doesn't mean, as some claim, that Jesus became "a putrefying mass of sin." Had this been possible, it would have done nothing for the sinner. *"For us"* means that God did everything to release us from sin by causing His Son to bear *"the sin of many"*[19] and by *"cancelling the record of debt that stood against us,"* which He achieved by *"nailing it to the cross."*[20] God made Him to be sin in the sense that He became our sin offering, and two great needs were satisfied at once. The demands of God's holiness were fully met. His wrath toward sin was diverted, and His wrath toward sinners was averted for those who believe.

This means that the Lord Jesus Christ became *"a propitiation"* by satisfying God's holy requirement through His precious blood that appeases His wrath. Some versions use the word *"expiation,"* but this refers to the other great need that He accomplished through the same precious blood that cleanses us from sin. At present, individuals come to Christ and become members of His body, because God and they have been satisfied. To purchase His bride, Jesus paid the debt by His blood, and this is what Paul meant when he wrote, *"Christ also loved the church and gave Himself for her."*[21] In the future, when Christ comes to the air, He will take them Home to be with Him forever.[22] The church will be with its Builder, the body will be with its Head, and the bride will be with her Bridegroom.

Every Bible subject is worthy of study, but apart from knowing God – Father, Son and Holy Spirit in all Their delightful attributes – we will search long to find one so glorious as the bride of Christ. For this reason, it merits much more than minimalist treatment, not least since God has given it bible-wide coverage. He has much to say about it, therefore we have much to learn as our Teacher, the Spirit of glory, leads us step by step into something so grand in its exaltation of the glory of Christ and the glory of God. The bride is described as *"a glorious church"* in Ephesians 5:27, and our present appreciation of our beloved Bridegroom will stir our affection for Him and heighten our anticipation of being with Him.

Our study is intentionally detailed and calls for patient and careful consideration. God has sown His purpose widely throughout His Word, and our prayer is that we will profit deeply as we reap.

> More about Jesus let me learn,
> More of His holy will discern;
> Spirit of God my teacher be,
> Showing the things of Christ to me.
> *(Eliza Edmunds Hewitt)*

HALLELUJAH! GOD ALONE!

Never, through eternal ages, in the vastness of the past,
    While creating things in heaven and the earth,
Did the Master-workman summon from the great angelic host[1]
One to help Him bring these wondrous works to birth?

His the Mastermind that planned them in the Triune Deity;
    His the craftsmanship that formed them by a word;[2]
God – the Father, Son and Spirit – They alone work wondrously,[3]
    In Their own unique authority as LORD.[4]

But another wonder waited in the mystery of Christ,
    In the incarnation of the Holy One:
A woman was the vessel by whom His will would be sufficed,
    And such Infant holiness was *"to be born."*[5]

His humanity and Deity blended as *"the Child grew"*[6]
    And the body God prepared for Him was seen[7]
To comply with laws of nature; yet the One whose name is Love[8]
    Showed His spirit, wisdom, grace, were from above.

Thus His life on earth divulges something never seen in heav'n
    Where His loftiness and glory shone instead;[9]
On the pathway to the Cross in which the Lamb of God was giv'n,
    To the place where *"He must go"*, there *"He was led."*[10]

Yes, *"it pleased the LORD to bruise Him"* in His predetermined will,[11]
    That the long-planned work of grace could be revealed[12]
To the hearts of those whose sinfulness He carried on that hill,
    While condemning others guilty – *"whom you killed."*[13]

Then the awe-inspiring moment where no hand could intervene,
They had *"led"*, but could not help to save *"His own"*;[14]
Others *"laid"* him in a tomb in which no other corpse had been,[15]
And *"God raised Him"* – Hallelujah! He alone![16]

1. Prov.8:27-30 2. Ps.33:6,9 3. Ps.72:18 4. Mal.3:6; 1 Cor.12:3; 2 Cor.3:17 5. Lk.1:35 6. Lk.2:40 7. Heb.10:5 8. 1 Jn 4:8,16 9. Is.6:1 10. Matt.16:21; Is.53:7 11. Acts 2:23 12. Is.53:10 13. Acts 10:39 ESV 14. Jn 1:11; 10:3,4 15. Mk.6:29; Jn 19:41 16. Acts 13:30

2

EVE: A BRIDE THROUGH BLOOD

"And the LORD God caused a deep sleep to fall on Adam, and he slept; and He took one of his ribs, and closed up the flesh in its place. Then the rib which the LORD God had taken from man He made into a woman, and He brought her to the man. And Adam said: "This is now bone of my bones and flesh of my flesh; she shall be called Woman, because she was taken out of Man." Therefore a man shall leave his father and mother and be joined to his wife, and they shall become one flesh" (Gen.2:21-24).

Toward the end of 2016, a new word was added to the Oxford Dictionary. It was 'post-truth,' and the definition given was – "Relating to or denoting circumstances in which objective facts are less influential in shaping public opinion than appeals to emotion and personal belief. e.g. 'In this era of post-truth politics, it's easy to cherry-pick data and come to whatever conclusion you desire.'" This is deceitful for it implies that how we feel and what we think are more important than what is true! But the concept is not as new as 2016; it began in the Garden of Eden.

As we begin to think about 'Seeing the bride in all the Scriptures,' God introduces it to us in the time of pre-deception.[1] This was an invaluable move on His part, particularly since it draws a distinct line between the era of perfection, when He opened Adam's side and saw the blood of the Bridegroom, and the era of post-truth imperfection when He saw the blood of the offering that clothed them. So we begin our walk by going into *"the garden of God"*[2] to see Jehovah Elohim, the triune God, at work as He says, *"Let Us make man in Our image."*[3] By Their power, *"The first man Adam became a living being."*[4] A direct translation of the Greek text puts it this way: "so and it is written, was made the first man Adam into a soul living," which tells us that Adam was created as a living soul. The next part of v.45 is very different: it translates as "the last Adam into a spirit quickening," but does not include the word for *"became,"* which is in italics in some English versions to show that it should not be in the text and to emphasise that the Lord Jesus Christ was not created. So it would be wrong to say He "was made." He came, but never "became"! In His incarnation and resurrection, He did what He always was as a life-giver. The contrast is stark, if we say that Adam was 'a getter' and Jesus is 'a Giver'!

Although Adam was perfect, he was lonely in his perfectness until God said, *"I will make a helper comparable to him."*[5] Without doubt, she can be included in Solomon's declaration about God, *"He has made everything beautiful in its time,"*[6] and we can be certain that Eve's perfection meant she was beautiful inwardly in her nature and outwardly in her demeanour. Together they mirrored each other's perfect character: in their activity, beauty, honesty, humility, integrity, purity, responsibility and spirituality, and all their features demonstrate that they were made in the image of God. Ephesians 5:27 speaks of the bride of Christ in her perfection, so we know that she also will be beautiful, and Paul describes this by saying, *"as we have borne the image of the earthy, we shall also bear the image of the heavenly."*[7] The earthy image is the opposite of God's, and this is seen in Genesis chapter 3 where Satan took command and sin affected the woman, and then the man, in their subjection to God. This reversed the original order of God first, then the man, followed by the woman, and the serpent last. Two things are worth noting:

*God put Adam into a deep sleep

This tells us three important things about Adam while God went about His work of forming a bride for him:

1. He didn't suffer;
2. She was made at no cost to him;
3. He did not consciously wait for her to be brought to him.

How different this is from the last Adam who was fully conscious throughout His sufferings! He knew exactly why He was suffering and for whom He was suffering, and what would be the eternal outcome, and is now consciously waiting for His bride to come to His side. This is made clear in the letter to the Hebrews. Chapter 9:26 tells us, *"He has appeared to put away sin by the sacrifice of Himself"* and then we read in chapter 10:12,13, *"But this Man, after He had offered one sacrifice for sins forever, sat down at the right hand of God, from that time waiting ..."* Between those two great statements, chapter 9:28 gives this wonderful assurance, *"To those who eagerly wait for Him He will appear a second time, apart from sin, for salvation."* Adam didn't suffer, because suffering never came in until after he and Eve had sinned. It was then everything changed, and all the changes brought consequences that the Lord endured in His sufferings.

- **SORROW**: "I will greatly multiply your sorrow" ... "A Man of sorrows" (Gen.3:16; Is.53:3,10; Matt.26:38; Heb.5:7);
- **PAIN**: "In pain you shall bring forth children" ... "Christ also suffered for sins" (Gen.3:16; 1 Pet.3:18);
- **THORNS**: "Both thorns and thistles it shall bring forth" ... "twisted a crown of thorns" (Gen.3:18; Mk.15:17-19);
- **SWEAT**: "In the sweat of your face" ... "And being in agony ... Then His sweat ..." (Gen.3:19; Lk.22:44);
- **BREAD**: "you shall eat bread ..." ... "He took bread, gave thanks and broke it" (Gen.3:19; Lk.22:19);
- **DEATH**: "You shall not eat it, nor shall you touch it, lest you die" ... "Christ died for us" (Gen.3:3,19; Rom.5:8)
- **SEPARATION**: "the LORD God sent him out" ... "He drove out" ... "[He] went out" ... "outside the gate" (Gen.3:23,24; Jn 19:17; Heb.13:12).

God took one of his ribs

The Hebrew word for *"ribs"* is *tsela,* which means the side, so it's possible that more than the actual rib was taken before God *"closed up the flesh in its place."* One commentator says, "Hebrew, *tsela,*a rib, more frequently the side, and accordingly, the Septuagint version renders it by *pleura,* a piece of his side" (Jamieson, Faussett, and Brown). This implies that God saw the blood of the perfect Bridegroom in chapter 2 before He saw the blood of the animal in chapter 3:21 for two imperfect sinners. This means that the adversary could never accuse Him of having an afterthought, once they had sinned, for the promise of the bride was revealed before the provision of coats of skin. So the companion was foreshadowed before the covering! This was essential, since the foreshadowing of *"the marriage of the Lamb"*[8] for those who are *"chosen in Christ before the foundation of the world"*[9] preceded the portrayal of *"the Lamb slain from* the foundation of the world."[10]

The bride through blood was provided in the purpose of God before Adam sinned and points forward to God's planned escape from the result that *"in Adam all die."*[11] In the garden of Eden, one sacrifice covered two sinners, which is confirmed by the word for *"clothed"* – *wayal^{e}bishēm* – being singular and *kāt^{a}nōt ōr* for *"tunics"* or *"coats of skin"* with *ōr* also being singular. One offering provided one covering for both. In this way, God pointed forward to the cross of His Son where *"one sacrifice'* provides one covering for all.

From this rib, or side, God *"made"* the woman, and the Hebrew word *bānāh* means that He built her, which specifically points to the Saviour's words, *"I will build My church."*[12] Then He *"brought her to the man."* This means He led her to him. For Adam, Eden's perfect creation now had Eden's perfect companion to seal Eden's perfect completion; and the man who had perfect authority over all flesh now had perfect affection for his bride. No wonder Genesis 1:31 stands out from all the previous *"good"* days of creation, as God declared the sixth day to be *"very good."* What a day it was, with a perfect bride being brought to a perfect bridegroom for the first and last time! No vows were made, since perfection needs no vow to keep the bond on track.

The real beauty of this union is captured in the original language of Genesis 5:2 which some English versions translate as, *"Male and female created he them, and called their name Adam, in the day when they were created."* Having joined the singular *"male"* and the singular *"female,"* God then refers to the plural *"them ... their ... they"* before uniting them in the singular name, *"Adam."* How accurate are the shadows that God gives in His Word for, having united the first Adam and his bride in his name, God already knew that He would unite the last Adam and

His bride in His Name (*ho Christos*) – *"the Christ."* This is a uniquely honoured distinction for the church, which is His body, and we will look more closely at this particular aspect in our later consideration of such Scriptures as 1 Corinthians 12:12 and Ephesians 3:4.

All this is in harmony with the Gospel of Christ which promises, *"All that the Father gives Me will come to Me, and the one who comes to Me I will by no means cast out."*[13] The Lord used two words – *"all,"* meaning the church; and *"the one,"* meaning each member. He will *"raise it"* (the church) and *"raise him"* (the member) ... *"and no one can come to Me unless the Father who sent Me draws him."*[14] By saying this, the Lord Jesus Christ continued to weave the great truth of His church into John's Gospel record in support of John's comment in chapter 3:29 – *"He who has the bride is the bridegroom; but the friend of the bridegroom, who stands and hears him, rejoices greatly because of the bridegroom's voice"* - just as He did in Matthew 16:18 by referring to building His church. John leaves us in no doubt that he has recognised Christ as the Bridegroom by going on to say these momentous words, *"He must increase, but I must decrease."*

The mystery and manifestation

Paul spoke about *"the mystery"* that had been *"kept secret since the world began."*[15] He also wrote about *"the mystery which has been hidden from ages and from generations, but now has been revealed to His saints,"*[16] yet there's no doubt that the Old Testament and the Gospels hold rich teaching about it. This helps us to understand that the real meaning of the word *"mystery"* (Gr. *mustērion*) is not something so obscure that it's never understood, but something God makes known to His own as part of revealing His Son.[17] This is clearly borne out by the following Scriptures:

*"And **to make all men see** what is the dispensation of the mystery which from all ages hath been hid in God who created all things"* (Eph.3:9 RV).

*"... the mystery kept secret since the world began but now made manifest, and by the prophetic Scriptures **made known to all nations**, according to the commandment of the everlasting God, for obedience to the faith"* (Rom.16:25,26).

*"The mystery which has been hidden from ages and from generations, but **now has been revealed to His saints**"* (Col.1:26).

How wonderful this is! Whilst being hid from men, it was hid in God; and being kept from men, it was kept by God until He would let it be *"made known"* among *all men* and *all nations* to those who would be *His saints*. John combines with Paul to highlight the great truth of the sovereignty of God while, at the same time, underlining man's responsibility. In the perfect will of God, the Father *"gives"* and *"draws,"* the sinner *"comes,"* *"the one"* becomes an indivisible part of the *"all,"* and each knows that the Lord will raise both *"him"* and *"it"* at His coming. The New Testament broadens this theme by describing the mystery in three ways:

1. A **building** > *Construction* > United with the **Rock** > Made to last;
2. A **body** > *Coordination* > United with the **Head** > Made to live;
3. A **bride** > *Communion* > United with the **Bridegroom** > Made to love.

The testimony of Genesis 2:24 is that Adam was *"joined to his wife,"* in a bond that implies he would stick to her in their God-given relationship. It's such a strong word [Heb. *dābaq*] that the noun *debeq* is used in

Isaiah 41:7 for *"soldering"* – an extremely strong bond, which is carried forward into Ephesians 5 to show how such a bond manifests itself.

Subjection & Submission
v.24, *"so let the wives be to their husbands in everything."*
If not, then she is not a good wife!

Sensitivity & Support
v.29, *"nourishes ... cherishes"* (i.e. cares and pampers)
If not, then he is not a good husband!

Separation & Sanctification
v.31, *"two shall become one"*
If not, then it is not a good marriage!

In marriage, these characteristics reflect what the bride is to Christ, and what He is to His bride, as the following verses show.

Provider and Preserver – He is the Saviour of the body (v.23)

The Builder who provides the bond also protects it, and a husband should reflect this in the care he provides for his wife in forming their marriage and by how he protects her from then on to ensure that their marriage 'works.' He can fail to fulfil this analogy, but the Saviour who provides perfect salvation for individual believers cannot fail to protect the overall perfection of His church.

However, His protection goes farther than maintaining its formation, He also protects its function through the *"working"*[18] of every part and in the diversity of gift as God *'works all in all.'*[19] In His own unique way, He also protects the witness of the church – *"to the principalities and powers in the* heavenly places, according to the eternal purpose which He accomplished in Christ Jesus our Lord,"[20] while, at the same time, safeguarding her subjection.[21] These concepts are vitally important, and we can trace them back to the essential nature of our bond with Christ who is *"head over all things to the church, which is His body, the fulness of Him who fills all in all."*[22] As His *"fulness,"* His church doesn't merely supplement Him, it is the complement of Him, and this lofty thought should ensure that we give as much attention to the end of Ephesians chapter 1 as we do to the end of chapter 2. What we are *in* Him must always shape what He wants us to be *for* Him!

Purchaser - Christ also loved ... and gave Himself for her (v.25)

The wonder of the gospel is that God gave His Son and the Son gave Himself. How true it is that each believer rests securely in the unassailable belief that He *"gave Himself for me,"*[23] but it is equally true that He *"gave Himself for her."* Through His death, each member has been *"bought with a price,"*[24] and so has the church in her entirety.

Purifier - He might sanctify and cleanse (v.26)

The moment of salvation brings the same assurance that the Lord gave to eleven disciples in the Upper Room: *"you are clean."*[25] This is what His precious blood has secured in our redemption. When speaking to Nicodemus, the Lord talked about being *"born of water,"*[26] and this is what He secures through His Word as the Holy Spirit shares it with convicted sinners. Jesus went on to tell Nicodemus, *"We speak what We know and testify what We have seen,"*[27] for They both speak the Word, and so does the Father for *"He brought us forth by the word of truth."*[28] Having granted us spiritual wealth through the Word as sinners, God also grants us spiritual health through *"the implanted word"*[29] as believers.

Alongside this great truth, our salvation was applied *"in sanctification of the Spirit"*[30] and, having begun this way with individuals, the Lord, as Bridegroom, has sanctified and cleansed His church through the self-same Word. Both Greek words are in the aorist tense to signify they are already done, though it's interesting to note that the word *"and"* doesn't come between them in the Greek language. It simply says, *"sanctify cleanse,"* perfectly made ready in holiness for the Holy One! This is the great triumph of the cross that He accomplished the purchase of His bride through providing our atonement, purified her by His word and is ready to welcome her Home to heaven that ...

Presenter - He might present her (v.27)

The Greek word *parastēsē* indicates that she will not stand before Him or behind Him for He will welcome her to stand **beside** Him in glory. By reconciling us *"in the body of His flesh through death,"* the bridegroom has made Himself ready to present us, and the marvel is He has made us ready to be presented *"holy, and blameless, and above reproach in His sight."*[31] The one who *"stood by"* Paul, and many believers since, will cause us to stand by Him and will present us to Himself. It will be His own personal honour. Our relationship with Him began on earth, because *"He Himself has suffered";*[32] it continues on earth, because *"He Himself has said";*[33] and it will have its climax in heaven when He alone – and who is more fitted? – will *"present (us) to Himself."*

THE GOSPEL

Its fundamental doctrines gleam afar;
Eternal in the heavens is their source; (1:1)
Each penetrates our darkness like the star
That sets the boatman's sextant and his course.

*

Its monumental witness towers above
All earthly concepts, helping us to find
Deep thoughts of God, and evidence of love,
In nobler thoughts shaped in His noblest mind.

*

Invisible, yet by His works made known, (1:20)
This all-creating God is clearly seen;
His hidden things are manifestly shown, (16:25-27)
Revealed in time His everlasting plan.

*

Our non-judgmental God has made us free (8:2)
From sin's dark presence, penalty and pow'r.
And now electing grace calls us to be (8:29)
Conformed to His Son's image hour by hour.

*

Since death has lost its lordship over Him, (6:9)
And having died to death He dies no more;
So, under grace, we live as dead to sin: (6:11)
Its lordship gone from those whose sins He bore. (6:14)

3

REBEKAH: A BRIDE THROUGH THE SPIRIT

"Now Abraham was old, well advanced in age; and the LORD had blessed Abraham in all things. So Abraham said to the oldest servant of his house, who ruled over all that he had, "Please, put your hand under my thigh, and I will make you swear by the LORD, the God of heaven and the God of the earth, that you will not take a wife for my son from the daughters of the Canaanites, among whom I dwell; but you shall go to my country and to my family, and take a wife for my son Isaac." And the servant said to him, "Perhaps the woman will not be willing to follow me to this land. Must I take your son back to the land from which you came?" But Abraham said to him, "Beware that you do not take my son back there. The LORD God of heaven, who took me from my father's house and from the land of my family, and who spoke to me and swore to me, saying, 'To your descendants I give this land,' He will send His angel before you, and you shall take a wife for my son from there. And if the woman is not willing to follow you, then you will be released from this oath; only do not take my son back there" (Gen.24:1-8).

We were leaving the funeral service for the burial when the driver of the funeral director's car slid back the glass partition and asked, "What do you think of Genesis 22, 23 and 24?" My answer was, "I've been helped to see that God was painting a picture in these three chapters: in chapter 22, of Isaac on the altar and the provision of a substitute; in chapter 23, the death of Sarah; and in chapter 24, we find a bride being brought home for Isaac. All three foreshadow the purpose of God in Christ: chapter 22, points to His death on the cross as our Substitute; chapter 23, represents the setting aside of Israel; and chapter 24, points forward to the bride of Christ being brought Home." The driver replied, "Yes, that's what I was thinking," and closed the partition.

Pictures abound in Genesis. For example, we have just considered the Divine wisdom that began to unveil His eternal purpose in the church, which is the body of Christ by foreshadowing the shedding of His blood in Genesis 2:7 and 3:21 as God saw the blood of the Bridegroom before shedding the blood of the sacrifice. It's also worth seeing that He portrayed a bride through blood in the garden of God before portraying one in the city of God through the outpouring of His Spirit. Moriah was the place of sacrifice in Genesis 22 before it became the place of satisfaction in service, and God says of that place in Psalm 46:4, *"There is a river whose streams shall make glad the city of God, the holy place of the tabernacle of the Most High."* By combining these two, He was pointing forward to the work of the cross and to the Day of Pentecost, so that the covering of the sinner and the calling of the sinner would be accomplished.

Iraq to Jerusalem is a long way to walk, yet this is the road we must travel if we want to see what was involved in bringing home a bride for Isaac. By the time chapter 24 opens, Abraham and Isaac have been linked with four great landmarks, each with its own special meaning for them, and for believers in Christ.

Hebron

First mentioned in Genesis 13:18, its name reminds us of God's desire for fellowship [Heb. from *chābar*: joined, coupled, fascinated], which isn't achieved by force, but by fascination.

Jerusalem

Introduced to us as Salem in Genesis 14:18 when Melchizedek met with Abram, and confirmed as Jerusalem in Psalm 76:1,2 as God's central place for service.

Moriah

As its name implies, this was the landmark chosen by God as the place that was seen by Jehovah where He would provide the sacrifice (see Ex.12:13 – *"when I see"* from the same word translated *"will provide"* in Gen.22:8), where the Temple would be built[1] and be in the same region as Calvary where the Lord Jesus Christ would be crucified.

Machpelah

The burial place in Genesis 23:9 was a place with two openings (Heb. *double*), as a sign that those who live by faith are promised a way in and a way out of death through the resurrection of Christ promised in 1 Corinthians 15:20 and 21.

Rebekah would never have known, but her calling resulted from Abraham and Isaac's association with these four places and, though she may have been told about them during her journey with the servant, they give us six things to think about in terms of actions, consequences and divine input:

1. **The father appealed** > *Revealing his will for his son* > The father's word (Jn 6:44);
2. **The bride attracted** > *Responding to the unseen and relying on the Word* > The Spirit's work (1 Pet.1:8; Rom.10:17);
3. **The substitute accepted** > *Reaching the stranger* > The Son's worth (2 Cor.5:21);
4. **The bride adorned** > *After the sacrifice of Moriah* > The Son's submission (Jn 17:4);
5. **The bride adorned** > *After going on the altar* > The son's obedience (Phil.2:8)
6. **The bride adorned** > *After the death of Sarah* > The gospel to the Gentiles (Rom.9:23,24).

Must I take your son back?

Abraham was very definite that the bride must come to the son, and that the son must not be taken to where she was. This fits well with our coming to Christ[2]. Rebekah must leave her place and go to Isaac's place, just as the bride of Christ will come out of the world to Him, for He will not go back into the world for her. Her response must be based on *"the hearing of faith,"*[3] not on sight. For a very different reason than Jephthah, Isaac could have said, *"I have opened my mouth unto the LORD, and I cannot go back."*[4]

Beware that you do not take my son back there

Abraham's choice of word could hardly have been stronger. By using the Hebrew *shāmar*, which means to guard or hedge about, as if with thorns, he emphasised that this command regarding his son must be protected, as if by an impermeable barrier. It was a very clear warning from him that Isaac must not go back to his pre-Moriah days. His steps would not be retraced, just as the cross cannot be repeated.

> Nevermore shall God the Father
> Smite the Shepherd with the sword;
> Ne'er again shall lawless sinners
> Set at nought the glorious Lord.
> (R.C. Chapman)

As a man of faith,[5] and *"father of all those who believe,"*[6] Abraham stood against the myth that seeing is believing. Rebekah would never be able to say, "I'll believe him if I see him," and she gives no support to those who say, "I'll believe it, if I see it." Unlike her, chief priests who ought to have known the truth did express this view when they said, *"Let the Christ, the King of Israel, descend now from the cross, that we may see and believe."*[7] Faith is believing without seeing,[8] and Rebekah's response was based entirely on what she heard, not upon what she saw. Time after time, the inspiration of Scripture is proved by the accuracy of complementary Old Testament shadows that link up with New Testament substance. It's as if the Lord's own principle in John 5:24 was sown into her life: *"Most assuredly, I say to you, he who hears My word and believes in Him who sent Me has everlasting life."* Not he who sees, but *"he who hears"*!

Having begun by *"the hearing of faith,"*[9] Rebekah continued to *"walk by faith"*[10] depending on nothing other than the servant's testimony about a father and his son. In a lovely way, the servant represents the essential nature of the Holy Spirit's witness, whose witness is equal to God the Father's and His Son's.

- John 3:11 - "We speak what We know ... Our witness": **THE SON & THE SPIRIT'S WITNESS**;
- John 8:18 - "I am the One who bears witness ... the Father ... bears witness of Me": **THE SON & THE FATHER'S WITNESS**;
- John 16:15 - "He will take of Mine and declare it to you": **THE SPIRIT'S WITNESS.**

Golden nose ring and two bracelets

Three things emerge from the servant's meeting and conversation with Rebekah. First, in verse 22, we see the bride's present; in verse 28, we see the bride's pleasure; and, finally, in verse 61 we see the bride's prospect. In all three, the servant portrays the Holy Spirit's ministry, of which Jesus said, *"He will glorify Me, for He will take of what is Mine and declare it to you,"*[11] and Rebekah depicts the believer's response to His working. By accepting the ring and bracelets, she received the tokens from the servant who recognised that he was speaking to the bride whom Abraham, the father, had described in verse 4. In this she foreshadowed believers in the Lord Jesus Christ who receive the gift of the Holy Spirit as "the guarantee" – the *"arrhabōn"* – the engagement ring or pledge of their spiritual inheritance and ultimate safe escort by Him *"until"* or, as the word *eis* indicates *"into the redemption of the purchased possession, to the praise of His* – that is, the Father's – *glory."*[12] Like the servant, the Spirit of God will guide us the whole way Home!

Rebekah's bridal pleasure is symptomatic of believers rejoicing in their anticipation of seeing and being at Home with their Bridegroom.[13] As far as she was concerned, her bridal union with the unseen Isaac was cause for newfound satisfaction and excitement, so she *"ran and told her mother's household these things"*[14] just as she *"ran back to the well to draw water"* at the unknown servant's request. When asked, *"Will you go with this man?"* she promptly said, *"I will go,"* and, to the end of the journey, she *"followed the man."* What a lesson for all of us! Having *"begun in the Spirit,"*[15] God's desire is that we will continue to be *"led by the Spirit of God"*[16] for the rest of our journey. He is the One through whom God spoke to us to bring us to Christ for salvation, and we gladly say to our Saviour, *"Draw me, we will run after thee."*[17] This is how we should begin, and Hebrews 12:1,2 urges to *"run with endurance the race that is set before us, looking unto Jesus."* What a way to end!

And what of her prospect? Do you not think her whole bridal journey was wrapped up in her longing to be with her bridegroom? Oh, it was one thing to hear of him and to learn more and more about him, but nothing would compare to being with him! Was her conversation not all about him in verse 61? Was her anticipation not all about seeing him in verse 64? And was her devotion not all for him in verse 65? Her final act before meeting him shows how fitting her readiness was for that special moment. It wasn't about her at all. It was all about him, *"So she took a veil and covered herself."* Here lies a vital reminder for us all: being our Bridegroom doesn't place us in a position of familiarity at the moment of His coming out to meet us. No, He is Jehovah the Saviour, the Lord of glory, worthy of all honour!

> What will it be to dwell above,
> And with the Lord of glory reign,
> Since the blest knowledge of His love
> So brightens all this dreary plain?
> No heart can think, no tongue explain,
> What joy 'twill be with Christ to reign.
> (J. Swain)

And Isaac ... lifted up his eyes

He had gone *"out to meditate in the field,"* but what was on his mind? Unlike our omniscient Saviour, he must have been asking himself, "What will she be like? Will she be enthralled by me? Will I be disappointed in her?" Shortly, he would find out, and that would be the end of the bridegroom's anticipation of her for, although he didn't know her, he would recognise her by what she was wearing: the ring and bracelets, the gold and silver jewellery, and the clothing that would mark her out as his. In some eastern marriage customs, the bridegroom sent a length of white cloth to his unseen bride, and when she arrived for their wedding ceremony he recognised her by the golden ornaments he had sent at regular intervals for her to attach to her bridal cloth. It would be like this for Isaac and Rebekah, and so it should be for us when we rise to meet our Saviour at His coming.

Then Rebekah lifted up her eyes

If ever there was harmony in a couple's affections, it was now, as Isaac *"lifted up his eyes"* and *"Rebekah lifted up her eyes."* In keeping with his anticipation of her, she showed her corresponding anticipation of him. She had heard of Isaac being in two places – on the altar and with his father – but now she saw him coming to meet her as his bride. All three are beautifully fulfilled as we view Christ in Hebrews 9 – on the cross in verse 26, with His Father in verse 24, and coming for His bride in verse 28. It seems highly unlikely that the servant would not have told her about Moriah to stir her initial appreciation of the one who was waiting for her to come to his side. It's also likely that he told her that Isaac was with his father *"and to him he has given all that he has."*[18]

Now, in her combined feelings of appreciation, admiration and attraction, she was about to meet him and to hear his voice, and the faith by which she had been walking gave way to sight. Leaving her camel, she moved toward him to discover that her shortest walk was the best one of all. She was home! Well might she have pre-empted Job's comment: *"I have heard of You by the hearing of the ear, but now my eye sees You."*[19] And she could have anticipated meeting him by saying, *"Whom I shall see for myself ... How my heart yearns within me!"*[20] With an even greater sense of expectation, the Christian is *"Looking for the blessed hope and glorious appearing of our great God and Saviour Jesus Christ,"*[21] and is only too happy to say, *"Amen. Come, Lord Jesus!"*[22]

His mother Sarah's tent

Sarah died between two great events: Isaac on the altar and a bride being brought for him, and these point forward, as we have already thought, to the setting aside of Israel in Romans 11:15. Paul asks the great question: *"For if their being cast away is the reconciling of the world, what will their acceptance be but life from the dead?"* Rebekah's new home was in the temporary dwelling of Isaac's mother's tent, but the church will be in the Father's house,[23] and the bride in her eternal home – *"So we are always confident, knowing that while we are at home in the body we are absent from the Lord. For we walk by faith, not by sight. We are confident, yes, well pleased rather to be absent from the body and to be present with the Lord."*[24]

Blessed Abraham ... blessed Rebekah (vv.1, 60)

The chapter begins with Abraham being blessed. It continues with Isaac being given "all *that he has"* and ends with Rebekah being blessed with present and future blessing. What a picture of believers being *"blessed with every spiritual blessing in the heavenly places in Christ,"*[25] presently and eternally! We shall meet Him, we will see Him whom not having seen we love, and we will hear His voice.

The funeral director's question is still worth asking. What do you think of Genesis 22, 23 and 24? How thankful we are that the Spirit of God helps us to answer it. Having foreshadowed a bride through blood in Genesis 2, we now trace the wonder of a bride through the Spirit portrayed in chapter 24. The first depicts a bride being bought; the second, a bride being brought, and only an all-knowing God could so specifically portray a bride for His Son in Genesis before urging us to look forward into the book of Exodus, and this we will do next.

Who is this who comes to meet me
On the desert way,
As the morning star foretelling
God's unclouded day?
He it is who came to save me
On the cross of shame;
In His glory well I know Him,
Evermore the same.

Oh, the blessed joy of meeting,
All the desert past!
Oh, the wondrous word of greeting
He shall speak at last.
He and I together entering
Those bright courts above;
He and I together sharing
All the Father's love.

He, who in the hour of sorrow
Bore the cross alone;
I, who through the lonely desert
Trod where He had gone;
He and I in that bright glory
One deep joy shall share –
Mine to be for ever with Him,
His that I am there.
(Emma Frances Bevan)

4

ISRAEL: A BRIDE FOR GOD

"And Moses brought the people out of the camp to meet with God ... Now this is what you shall offer on the altar: two lambs of the first year, day by day continually. One lamb you shall offer in the morning, and the other lamb you shall offer at twilight ... This shall be a continual burnt offering throughout your generations at the door of the tabernacle of meeting before the LORD, where I will meet you to speak with you. And there I will meet with the children of Israel, and the tabernacle shall be sanctified by My glory" (Ex.19:17; 29:38, 39, 42, 43).

Genesis is a book in which God dealt with individuals, and this includes women who still give a lovely foreshadowing of the bride. Exodus is different, just as the overall purpose of God moved on from those individuals to the formation of His people as a nation. The nearest we get to catching a glimpse of this unfolding purpose is in Genesis 49 when dear old Jacob gathered his twelve sons at his bedside for his parting blessing. It's only by looking back that we can link this family gathering around his bed to what God foresaw in twelve tribes becoming His family gathered around His tabernacle. We also find bridal resemblances in His relationship with them and, when we come to chapter 7, we will see how He does something very similar in the New Testament by applying the likenesses of the church to life in local assemblies. But to begin, we will look at two Old Testament examples of this: the first, here in Exodus; and the second, in the Song of Songs. Our opening reading speaks of God calling His people, and it's very specific as to 'where' and 'why.'

Out of the camp to meet with God

Meeting is a great experience. The book of Exodus speaks about the best kind of meetings, and there are two different descriptions of them. The first one in chapter 19:17 says, *"And Moses brought the people out of the camp to meet with God."* We can imagine a whole parade of people leaving their tents and walking in the same direction. If we could have asked some of them where they were going, everyone would have said the same thing: "I'm going to meet God." And what a meeting it was! It meant they had a real dealing (Heb. *qir'āh*: an encounter) with Him. So it was a very worthwhile meeting.

It's good that we take time to take in the progress God is making in painting these Old Testament bridal pictures. Firstly, in Genesis, He gave a bride in the garden of God; then He brought one to the city of God; and now, in Exodus, He brings His people to the mountain of God with a tremendous sense of anticipation. If we are being honest with ourselves, when last did we go to a gathering of the Lord's people with the same conviction that we were meeting Him? And when was the last time we left such a gathering knowing that we had experienced a real dealing with Him? The danger is that we have attended without being affected!

Paul was well aware of this great meeting in Exodus 19, and he sums up the contrast between the giving of the Old Covenant and the giving of the New Covenant in 2 Corinthians 3.

v.7 The ministry of death

He says it was *"glorious,"* while adding that the ministry of the Spirit is *"more glorious."* The Law focused on sin, yet it could never justify the sinner by pointing it out.[1] Nevertheless, its ministry was *glorious* for it revealed the holiness of God while convicting men of their sinfulness. The ministry of the Spirit focuses on forgiveness of sin and grants righteousness.[2] it not only reveals the holiness of God, but causes the believing sinner to share it in Christ, therefore it is *"more glorious."*

v.8 The ministry of condemnation

He says, *"had glory,"* while *"the ministry of righteousness exceeds much more in glory."* The Law convicted and condemned sinners of their sin, yet it had *"glory"* because it helped them to discover that they stood condemned before the holy nature of the Lawgiver. By contrast, the *"ministry of righteousness"* convicts and converts, and it *"exceeds much more in glory"* because believers, without works, are *"made righteous"*[3] and become *"partakers of the divine nature."*[4]

v.11 What is passing away

He says, it was *"glorious"*, but *"what remains is much more glorious."* The Old Covenant was rich in all these aspects of God's character: it was *"Holy ... spiritual ... righteous ... good,"*[5] for its high standards reflect the holiness, spirituality, righteousness, and goodness of God. It was all of these, because God is, and because this is how He wanted His people to be, yet He introduced a New Covenant that is *"better."*⁶

Where I will meet with you ... there I will meet

The next meeting is in chapter 29:38-43. God had just spoken about two lambs going on His altar, one in the morning and the other in the evening, then He said something very special: *"where I will meet you to speak with you. And there I will meet with the children of Israel."* How precious that was! They met with Him at the giving of the Law, and now He wanted to meet with them on the basis of the giving of the lamb. But this meeting was so different from the first that God used a different word to describe it. It was as if their regard for His Word needed to be combined with their relationship with the lamb, and He emphasised this with a word that refers to a couple getting engaged for marriage in Amos 3:3. *"Can two walk together, unless they are agreed?"* The Hebrew word *yāad* means to agree, but it can also refer to betrothal or being engaged.

God wanted them to know that His lambs were right at the heart of their relationship with Him and that living the Law would be much easier when coupled with loving the lamb. What a lovely way to walk with God! Would it not be, that minds set on the lamb in the morning and in the evening, would find it much easier to walk in His law as He wanted them to walk during the day? If we learn nothing else, the Holy Spirit would want us to sense the pulse of the heart of God revealed by coupling Law with the lamb, obedience with love, for they combine the Law of God and the grace of God. Grace will keep us from legalistic law-keeping, and the Law will keep us from a lethargic attitude to grace. He had made it clear in His law that their walk was of paramount importance to Him, and that blessing was promised on the basis of *"If you walk in My statutes and keep My commandments, and perform them."*⁷ However, He made it equally clear to them, if you *"walk contrary to Me, then I also will walk contrary to you."* But He had given two regulators to direct their will and their walk, their homes and their hearts, their actions and affections.

APPLICATION OF THE LAW & APPRECIATION OF THE LAMB

These go hand-in-hand and mutually enabled God's people to have a high regard for the Law and a holy relationship with Him through the lamb. This should have given each person the impetus to maintain obedience to the Law through love for the lamb while maintaining a love for the lamb through willing obedience to the Law. This is what God calls being *"obedient from the heart"*[8] in the New Testament. It means that love for the lamb should raise their esteem for the Law. It also means that it should have raised their resistance and reduced their threshold to sin.

In keeping with this, it should have governed those who judged sin, so that their judgment ensured the same high regard for the Law and the same holy relationship with the lamb. Godly administration must be conducted with loving care, not with legalistic coldness, and it should emphasise to offenders that they were judges on behalf of the Law and shepherds on behalf of the lamb. These are considerations that ought to have conditioned the minds and hearts of everyone who had the opportunity to meet with God. The thought of having an "encounter" with Him should have been enough to make this a reality, but coming to His meeting place at the altar in the bond of betrothal should have made it an absolute certainty. They should never be tainted as *"workers of iniquity"*;[9] they should never come under the influence of *"the throne of iniquity"*;[10] and their bridal bond with God should keep them from *"the bond of iniquity."*[11] To help His people in all this, God spelled out seven valuable features of this "agreement."

*Day by day continually

The law and the lamb were combined to foreshadow the Person of Christ, and such couplings are not uncommon in the Old Testament Scriptures. For instance, two tablets represented a whole Law,[12] and Isaiah 42:21 says of the Lord, *"He will exalt the law, and make it honourable."* Likewise, two sparrows associated with the cleansing of the leper in Leviticus 14:4, one killed and the other allowed to fly off, pointed to the death and resurrection of the Lord Jesus Christ. Two chapters later, two goats on the Day of Atonement combined to foreshadow Him again, as one was killed and the other led into a solitary place. This time, one represented Him who secured our atonement through His blood, and the other depicting Him as our sin-bearer in the most solitary place of all – the middle cross on Calvary.

*Morning and evening

Day after day, God's people woke to serve Him on the basis of what He had already received in the morning lamb; and night-by-night, as they went to sleep, the One who neither slumbers nor sleeps was left alone with the fragrance of the evening lamb as He watched over His dwelling place. What an appropriate reminder this is to us in our day that everything we offer is accepted on the basis of what Christ has already done!

God also said that the morning and evening sacrifices should be kept *"throughout your generations,"* and some events were highlighted by this timing. One lovely example was when David and the elders of Israel brought the ark of the covenant of the LORD from the house of

Obed-Edom with joy.[13] To his credit, he knew that God's joy was more important than theirs, and this meant doing what *"every day's work required."* The main focus of this was they began *"to offer burnt offerings to the LORD on the altar ... regularly every morning and evening ... according to ... the Law of the LORD which He commanded Israel."*[14] It was like an Old Testament version of the Lord's command in Matthew 28:18-20 that His disciples are asked to observe *"even to the end of the age."*

Elijah observed it, too, on Mount Carmel when victory over the prophets of Baal was *"At the time of the offering of the evening sacrifice."*[15] His successor, Elisha, was equally observant and equally victorious, and his triumph *"happened in the morning when the grain offering was offered.*[16] These occasions should make us thankful that things *"written before were written for our learning,"*[17] and we should allow the Spirit of God to teach us how important it is that the cross-work of our Lord Jesus Christ is at the forefront of all that we do. Apart from the actual principle involved, these days answered Exodus 29 in ways that distinctly pointed forward to the timing of the cross, and Mark gives the times that correspond to the morning and evening lambs in chapter 15:25 and 34 as the third and the ninth hour.

*A continual burnt offering

How fitting it is that the place of God's tabernacle, that speaks so beautifully of the Word who *"became flesh, and did tabernacle among us,"*[18] should have these two offerings that also speak wholly of Him set in place to mark the beginning and end of each day. Yes, we rightly delight in the Lamb who was slain for sinners, but these were wholly from God and for God,[19] and the people's offerings were accepted in between.

*Sanctified by My glory

Meeting with God is no small thing, and the bridal relationship He had for His people was no small thing either. He sealed it at the altar in the lambs that represented Christ in His death, and He sealed it again in the Most Holy Place where the ark of the testimony represented the living Christ exalted in glory. Once again, God said, *"And there I will meet with you, and I will speak with you from above the mercy seat, from between the two cherubim which are on the ark of the testimony."*[20] In a remarkable way, He again used the word *yāad* to show that their bridal bond was like a threefold cord inseparably uniting His place and their presentation with His presence. For us, too, these must go together, if the holiness of our daily walk is to be governed by our closeness to the Lamb and we are to be set apart untial, at last, we are *"raised in glory."*[21]

*The altar

God chose the place of sacrifice as the meeting ground, since coming there showed that it was the regulator of their lives, just as the work of the cross regulates our spiritual walk.[22] Other Scriptures emphasise that meeting with God on the basis of this marital pledge brought the people of God before Him in a special bond. He told them through Hosea, *"You will call Me "My Husband";*[23] and Isaiah's message was, *"Your Maker is your husband."* Later, God added, *"As the bridegroom rejoices over the bride, so shall your God rejoice over you."*[24] Through Jeremiah, God reminded them of how their relationship started: *"I remember you, the kindness of your youth, the love of your betrothal, when you went after Me in the wilderness."*[25]

During days when they were sliding toward captivity, this was a well-timed reminder of their deliverance from the bondage of Egypt through the blood of the Passover lamb, and their initial pledge of obedience at Sinai: *"All that the LORD has said we will do, and be obedient."*[26] Later again, God appealed to them through Ezekiel, saying, *"I washed you in water ... I anointed you with oil ... I clothed you ... I adorned you with ornaments, put bracelets on your wrists ... I put a jewel in your nose ... and a beautiful crown on your head."*[27]

His word through Ezekiel is reminiscent of Rebekah[28] and Ruth,[29] and we must pay attention to the divine order. There can be no anointing without washing, no clothing without anointing, and no adorning without clothing. For us, *"the washing of regeneration"*[30] must take place first, and it will be accompanied by *"an anointing,"*[31] and by a clothing and adorning that are both present and eternal.[32] My brothers and sisters, these two events in Exodus should make us long for something similar to happen among us.

- We need men who bring God's people out: and prevent us from *"forsaking the assembling of ourselves together, as is the manner of some."*[33]
- We need men who cause us to meet with God. Many men take meetings, but we need men who are empowered to take the people with them. First of all, they must hear God speaking to them, so that others will hear Him speak through them.
- We need men who help us enjoy the Word of God. Paul's urgent message is, *"Preach the Word!"*[34] It's not enough to give topical talks laced with anecdotes. Preachers should preach,[35] and teachers should expound – so they explore the Word and then explain the Word. Their motto should be 'Explore, Expand, Explain!'
- And we need men who help us to enjoy the Lamb. Our love for Him should be at the very core of the message. Those who listen should be able to hear how much we learn and how much we love.

When the preacher has finished his message, listeners should go home knowing they have not just been to a meeting. They should leave knowing they have been to meet with God. In Exodus 19 and 29, whether going to receive the Law or to value the lamb, there was one undeniable reality: there is a God. They had heard Him, and that was enough for faith to rest on an unshakeable foundation. In this assurance, we meet with Him.

IN CONTRAST
Wise, even in His foolishness,
And strong the weakness of His hand;
An endless deep His shallowness;
So vast, the tiniest things He planned.

Robust, yet veiled in gentleness,
And very God while truly Man;
He measures, yet is measureless,
With light years dwarfed within His span.

The Highest, in His lowliness;
Still Holy, though made sin for us,
And heaven's Best in emptiness
Dies with earth's worst upon a cross.

Engulfed in darkness is the Light,
And Love encounters hatred's power.
Heaven's Life expires within earth's night:
The Eternal One endures 'the hour.'

The Victim is the Victor now,

The One who died forever lives.
We gave our wickedness to Him:
His gentleness to us He gives.

As Love, He loves a loveless world;
As Friend, befriends a friendless earth;
And now the Bridegroom waits to show
His perfect bride His perfect worth.

5

THE SHULAMITE: A BRIDE FOR THE KING

"While the king is at his table, my spikenard sends forth its fragrance. A bundle of myrrh is my beloved to me, that lies all night between my breasts. My beloved is to me a cluster of henna blooms in the vineyards of En Gedi. The voice of my beloved! Behold, he comes leaping upon the mountains, skipping upon the hills. My beloved is like a gazelle or a young stag. Behold, he stands behind our wall; he is looking through the windows, gazing through the lattice. Until the day breaks and the shadows flee away, turn, my beloved, and be like a gazelle or a young stag upon the mountains of Bether. By night on my bed I sought the one I love; I sought him, but I did not find him. Until the day breaks and the shadows flee away, I will go my way to the mountain of myrrh and to the hill of frankincense" (S of S 1:12-14; 2:8, 9, 17; 3:1; 4:6).

This Song wafts into our Bible like a wonderfully refreshing echo of Genesis 5:2. There we find the first bride and bridegroom sharing the same name, as God blessed them *"and called their name Adam"* (ASV, KJV, RV). Here in *"The song of songs,"*[1] the bride similarly reflects her bridegroom's name, since Shulamite[2] is the feminine version of Solomon. Although around three thousand years apart, both couples point forward to the greater blessing of the church being called "the Christ" after Christ. Its study will amply reward the Christian, and cause us to sing:

> My heart is full of Christ and longs
> This glorious matter to declare!
> Of Him I make my loftier songs,
> I cannot from His praise forbear;
> My ready tongue makes haste to sing
> The glories of my heavenly King.
> (Charles Wesley)

But how do we respond to having such an honourable and lofty name? Well, perhaps we can learn from the Shulamite. As soon as she heard this name being applied to her, she asked, *"What would you see in the Shulamite – as it were the dance of two camps?"* Her modesty had already been voiced in chapter 1:5 and 6 – *"I am dark, but lovely ... like the tents of Kedar, like the curtains of Solomon. Do not look upon me, because I am dark."* On the one hand, she acknowledged how she resembled dark nomadic tents; but, on the other, was as beautiful, suitable and acceptable as the King's curtains. She really was asking, *"What would you see in **me**?"* Do you see me as I see me? Or do you see what he sees in me?

These are good questions for Christians to ask. Is there *"the dance of two camps"* in us, too? Whether the bride was referring to her own divided affections and actions or that God's people were divided into Israel and Judah, we don't know. What we do know is that we can be divided too. For instance, we might say, *"For I know that in me (that is, in my flesh)* *nothing good dwells,"*³ yet, seeing ourselves as Christ sees us, we can triumphantly add, *"I have been crucified with Christ; it is no longer I who live, but Christ lives in me"*⁴ and I am *"accepted in the beloved."*⁵ If you are asking, "What would you see in me?" let the answer be, "Not what you see in yourself, but how you are seen in Him!"

The king's immediate response was to address her as, *"O prince's daughter!"* elevating her to royal status, and by doing this we are reminded of the bridal content of Psalm 45:13, *"The royal daughter is all glorious within the palace."* Like her, the Shulamite has appropriate standing in the presence of her king with her beautiful feet. She belongs there, because he wants her to be. How typical this is of our King! It's wholly because of Him that we can say, *"we have peace with God through our Lord Jesus Christ, through whom we have access by faith into this grace in which we stand, and rejoice in hope of the glory of God."*⁶ And it is only because of Him, that He will be able to present His bride *"to Himself a glorious church."*⁷

Having gleaned these precious lessons, there is much more to take on board from The Song for it's a fascinating record of the Shulamite's bridal journey with her bridegroom. In spite of its ups and downs, he was able to tell her toward the end, *"How beautiful are your feet in sandals."*⁸ In this she resembles those who seek to win others for Christ as they *"preach the gospel of peace."*⁹ However, the last thing Solomon wanted was a barefooted bride, yet this is exactly what she was as night-time's shadows lengthened in chapter 5:3 when sandals were farthest from her mind and from her newly washed feet! This is another lesson we can learn from her, and there are many more, but who do the couple and their song represent? Some have suggested different ways of interpreting it and applying it:

1. The individual Jew's personal relationship with God;
2. Israel's collective national relationship with God;
3. The individual believer's relationship with Christ;
4. The church - the body's relationship with Christ;
5. It can be used for counselling Christian couples.

It's likely that the primary application is to Israel's collective relationship with God, yet it may well be that 'The Song' holds valuable lessons for each of the other four. Even so, it is hardly possible that divine inspiration caused such beautiful Hebrew poetry to be written for such a man-centred purpose as the last possibility. So it's better that we allow its language to lift our thoughts to see God being exalted in His relationship with His people, Israel, and His Son exalted as we draw lessons of Him and His church. One thing we learn right away is that the bride made a good start for her comments in chapter 1:13 and 14 sound like the testimony of *"first love."*[10] Let's trace her appreciation of her bridegroom as she speaks of four things.

My spikenard sent forth its fragrance

She had no doubt about where he was – *"the king is at his table"* – and like the woman who came to the Saviour in Mark 14:3, she came to his feet with her spikenard. The New Testament word is *pistikēs nardou*, which means genuine or faithful nard. We can look upon it as the fragrance of faith. It's interesting to note that He also was *"at the table,"* and both women knew that tables were for getting, yet they saw them as places for giving. The fragrance of their love offerings is like a song, as from their hearts they sang their silent duet. How beautifully they teach us how to approach *"the Lord's table"* Paul speaks of in 1 Corinthians 10:21, that, while coming to partake of it, we might come to give the fragrance of our worship of the King! Well might we say of Him and to Him, *"I will* sing unto the LORD as long as I live; I will sing praise to my God while I have my being. My meditation of him shall be sweet: I will be glad in the LORD."[11]

Paul also reminds us in 2 Corinthians 2:14 (NASB) that God *"always leads us in triumph in Christ, and manifests through us the sweet aroma of the knowledge of Him in every place."* There's no limit as to where we spread it: it's in every place, and disciples express the fragrance of faith in two ways – as witnesses in the outside place, and as worshippers in the Holy Place.[12] And, in a better way than these two women, we meet Him at *"the Lord's table."*[13]

> Much incense is ascending
> Before th 'eternal throne;
> God graciously is bending
> To listen to His own.
> Though feeble are our praises
> Christ adds His sweet perfume,
> And love the censer raises
> Their odours to consume.
> (Mrs Mary Peters)

A bundle of myrrh

This is often the symbol of suffering and, like no other beloved, ours became like a bundle of myrrh. Not just myrrh, but *a bundle!* But where did she keep it? Treasured possessions can be kept safe in many a place, unlike treasured affections that can be kept only in the heart, and she knew it. Oh, she says, it *"lies all night between my breasts"*; as if to confirm it's not a visitor, but a lodger that has come in permanently to stay. Christian, does your Saviour claim a similar place? His accumulated sufferings were varied: from hearing men's stinging words, as *"They* surrounded [Him] like bees"[14] to sinking in the "deep mire"[15] as He "bore our sins in His own body on the tree."[16] In answer to the myrrh, we see the bitterness of Marah in the Old Testament[17] and in the New Testament[18] where the Greek word *muron* is translated as "*ointment*" or "*oil*", and related to the word for myrrh, as in Smyrna the suffering church.

Like them, we also can enter into "*the fellowship of His sufferings*"[19] and know something of being "*bound in the bundle*" of His protecting sufferings. This Hebrew phrase, *ts^{a}rurāh bits^{e}rōr*, is achieved almost by duplicating the same word, and it was first used by Abigail when she so eloquently described David's inherent safety, because he was "*bound in the bundle of the living with the LORD.*"[20] How insightful! And the same can be said about believers in the Lord Jesus, but only because we are bound up, tied into, and wrapped up in the bundle of His sufferings.

A cluster of henna blooms

His sufferings meant that He fulfilled the underlying thought behind the word "*henna*," which comes from the Hebrew word, *kopher*, for a covering. This was demonstrated in a literal sense in Genesis 6:14 when Noah's ark was covered with a covering or pitched with pitch. This completely sealed the ark, making it watertight and able to withstand the buffeting of lashing waves, while effectively causing eight souls and all the livestock to be bound up in the bundle of its safety. However, it wasn't just "*henna*," it was "*a cluster of henna*"! From a spiritual point of view, her bunch of henna gathered together the different facets of atonement, purging, a ransom, reconciliation and forgiveness – to portray the full redemptive cost of our covering. We feel the weight of what we owe to our Sufferer and grasp the fragrance of His blood-bought forgiveness. What a bundle! What a cluster!

In the vineyards

But where could such symbols of redeeming grace be found? Surely, among those who were redeemed! Would another song not give the answer? *"Now let me sing to my Well-beloved a song of my Beloved regarding His vineyard: My Well-beloved has a vineyard on a very fruitful hill. He dug it up and cleared out its stones, and planted it with the choicest vine. He built a tower in its midst, and also made a winepress in it; so He expected it to bring forth good grapes, but it brought forth wild grapes. And now, O inhabitants of Jerusalem and men of Judah, judge, please, between Me and My vineyard what more could have been done to My vineyard that I have not done in it"*[21]

Yes, this was the place: in the citadel of the king, and among his kingly people, but, instead of being the productive vintage at the fountain of En Gedi, their condition was more like the nearby Dead Sea. Well, there were times when the bride would be like this, too, but for now she wants to tell where she is in her relationship with him. For her, the vineyards speak of the joy and pleasure she has in thinking about her beloved and, later, when she walks with him in the vineyards, she may have drawn his attention to some henna flowers and told him what she thought. It was the perfect opportunity in a moment of corresponding desire for four times he had said, *"Return,"* and four times she replied, *"Let us."*[22]

Yes, there are times when our Beloved makes a similar appeal and patiently waits for a willing response. There was no force in The Song, and there is no force with the Saviour. He draws, that we might walk with Him when He wants, where He wants, and as He wants. It's in the heart's appreciation of His sufferings that we respond to redeeming love by walking in the fruitfulness of *"righteousness and peace and joy in the Holy Spirit."*[23]

Until the day breaks

Relationships have highs and lows; and friendships fluctuate when uncertainty cripples the present and clouds the future. The Shulamite suffered from this, and her relationship also suffered, just as Israel's changing condition damaged her bridal relationship with God. In contrast to their mercurial experience, the Lord's assurance regarding His church will never change for He has said, *"All that the Father gives Me will come to Me."*[24] This gives absolute certainty to all who receive Him as their Lord and Saviour, and allows us to say with confidence, *"And so we have the prophetic word confirmed, which you do well to heed as a light that shines in a dark place, until the day dawns and the morning star rises in your hearts."*[25]

Let's look at this more closely. God loves to confirm His Word or, as the King James Version says, He has given us *"a more sure word of prophecy."* It's not just sure, it is *"more sure,"* so there's no room for doubt. Paul agrees wholeheartedly with Peter and, using thoughts based on the same word (Gr. *bebaioteron*) helps us to see that by receiving *"the grace of God ... the testimony of Christ was confirmed in you,"* and then he adds, *"who will also confirm you to the end."*[26] It was confirmed at the beginning in their salvation, and He will confirm it to the end when *"the day dawns"* and Christ returns for His church.

> We wait to see the Morning Star appearing
> In glory bright.
> This blessed hope illumes with beams most cheering,
> The hours of night.
> (Miss Carson)

Night-time was a dark place for the bride in The Song, and she was looking for the morning to chase away her self-inflicted shadows. There's no doubt she had a desire to see him, but it was on her terms. Had he not just shown his desire for her and made an appeal that she could quote word for word? He had asked her to *"Rise up ... and come away,"* yet she remained unmoved. He then appealed to her sense of seeing, hearing, smell and taste, but she remained untouched. He wanted her to let him see her face and to let him hear her voice, yet she chose to remain hidden and silent. Even the offer of help to *"Catch us the foxes, the little foxes that spoil the vines"* didn't jolt her into action. Foxes are destructive, and so are little foxes that have their whole future ahead of them, but not even her sense of obligation was moved!

Only after he had gone did she do what we would call 'a double take,' and suddenly she felt she had the right to appeal to him. *"Until the day breaks and the shadows flee away, turn my beloved and be like a gazelle or a young stag upon the mountains of Bether."* Having just spurned all his efforts and his appeal, she now expects him to do it all again and surmount her 'Mountains of Separation.' How fickle the human heart is! She had no qualms about putting the onus on him, even though he had just numbered the peaks of separation in her five unresponsive senses, and named a sixth in not being responsible for getting rid of her *"little foxes."*

As far as our own lives are concerned, the Lord wants us to be both responsive and responsible, but this doesn't exclude His gracious willingness to help us overcome the things that separate us from Him and spoil the things that are for Him. The bridegroom in The Song gives a lovely example of this when he used the bride's own words as the basis of his later appeal. This time, he showed that he had a desire for her, and that it would rest on his terms. She had wanted him to dispel her separation by accepting her way to restored fellowship, but now he wants her to accept his way to restored fellowship by visiting the place of his choice: *"Until the day breaks and the shadows flee away, I will go my way to the mountain of myrrh and the hill of frankincense."* She had a bundle of myrrh, but he had a mountain of myrrh that was both a mountain of bitterness and a hill of sweetness. This was his way to renewed fellowship, and it would seem they point us, as God would also direct His people Israel, to the sorrows and sweetness of the cross where the Saviour went through infinitely more suffering than we could ever know about.

Calvary was both for the Lord. From birth to death, myrrh was associated with His deep suffering and with the steep *"mountain"* He had to ascend.[27] At the same time, frankincense refers to the fragrance that ascended to God from Him as the accepted Sacrifice.[28] From this aspect of His offering, Calvary was a *"hill"* He went up in the full joy and satisfaction of what He would accomplish.[29] We may even think of how we, as lost sinners, were identified with the sufferings of the cross; yet, as worshippers, are united in the sweetness of the One who was *"an offering and a sacrifice to God for a sweet-smelling aroma."*[30] This mountain of myrrh and hill of frankincense was the place where He gave complete satisfaction to God, and the place through which He shares this satisfaction with all who believe. They represent the suffering and glory of the Saviour, which contrast with one another while being inseparable and complementary, and both Testaments in our Bibles testify to this harmony in bringing us to know Him.

- He is the Rock for the building - **Under us**;
- He is the Head of the body - **Over us**;
- He is the Bridegroom for the bride - **Beside us**.

And we will walk with Him *"Until the day breaks."*

It was on another night-time that thoughts of her beloved stirred her heart, causing it to *"awake"*, and the very idea of his hand being on the latch of her door led her to say the essential words he was longing to hear, *"My heart was moved for him."*[31] At last, she was moved where it matters most for, if the heart is moved, the feet are sure to follow! The Song of Songs is a delightful part of God's Word and worthy of our closest attention, but perhaps the bride's most delightful phrase was when she said, *"My beloved is to me."*[32] As we move on to think of another Bible bride, let's take this phrase with us, so that we might look at the Lord Jesus Christ, our Bridegroom, and have more and more reason to say, *"My beloved is to me."*

NO CROSS?

Is the Monarch kingdom-less, (Col.1:13)
And His sheep still in distress?
Can the Bread no longer feed, (Jn 6:35)
Reaching sinners in their need?
Could His purpose turn to loss?
Only if there is no cross!

Has the Shepherd lost His flock; (Jn 6:39)
Left them stranded from the Rock?
Has the Bridegroom failed His bride, (Jn 3:28,29)
Estranged forever from His side?
Do they constant fret and toss?
Only if there is no cross!

No, His kingdom is secured, (2 Pet.1:11)
And His sheep are well-assured
That the Living Bread still feeds (Jn 6:51)
Every sinner that He leads.

Took their alloy, purged their dross, (Is.1:25)
Only since there is a cross!

Now the Shepherd shows His choice (Jn 10:14,27)
In His flock who know His voice;
And He calls them as His bride, (Jn 3:29)
Loved and longed for, to His side. (Eph.5:27)
Shown His great desire for us
Only in and through His cross!

6

RUTH: A BRIDE THROUGH REDEMPTION

"Then Boaz said to Ruth, 'You will listen, my daughter, will you not? Do not go to glean in another field, nor go from here, but stay close by my young women. Let your eyes be on the field which they reap, and go after them. Have I not commanded the young men not to touch you? And when you are thirsty, go to the vessels and drink from what the young men have drawn.' Now Boaz said to her at mealtime, 'Come here, and eat of the bread, and dip your piece of bread in the vinegar.' So she sat beside the reapers, and he passed parched grain to her; and she ate and was satisfied, and kept some back.

Then Naomi her mother-in-law said to her, 'My daughter, shall I not seek security for you, that it may be well with you? Now Boaz, whose young women you were with, is he not our relative? In fact, he is winnowing barley tonight at the threshing floor. Therefore wash yourself and anoint yourself, put on your best garment and go down to the threshing floor; but do not make yourself known to the man until he has finished eating and drinking. Then it shall be, when he lies down, that you shall notice the place where he lies; and you shall go in, uncover his feet, and lie down; and he will tell you what you should do.' And she said to her, 'All that you say to me I will do.'" So she went down to the threshing floor and did according to all that her mother-in-law instructed her. And after Boaz had eaten and drunk, and his heart was cheerful, he went to lie down at the end of the heap of grain; and she came softly, uncovered his feet, and lay down" (Ruth 2:8, 9, 14; 3:1-7).

If judgment can be described as God's *"strange work,"*[1] what might be said about the working of His grace? In some ways, we may say that it, too, can be strange. It was from the first bridegroom's wounded side that God formed his bride in the Garden of God; it was after the second bridegroom had been bound on an altar on Moriah that God brought his bride to him in what would become the city of God; and then He shared His bridal intent with the twelve tribes at Sinai, the mountain of God. Having gathered them together to His Name, the Song of Songs, as we have thought, can be viewed as an allegory of Israel in her bridal role as the people of God.

Moab

And now we come to consider Ruth the Moabitess. If God's delivering grace to Abraham took him from *"the other side of the River"* (Euphrates) where his family *"served other gods";*[2] if He had likewise freed Rebekah from her family among whom her brother, Laban, had *"gods";*[3] and if He had rescued His people from *"all the gods of Egypt,"*[4] it will be no surprise that Ruth also came from a background that was questionable from the start. Lot had two sons by incestuous birth, one of whom was Moab,[5] and the nation that came from him became an ungodly people on the eastern side of the Dead Sea. It was there that Ruth was reared, and she would have known about the national hostility between her country and Israel,[6] so she would be well aware that their God caused them to say, *"Woe to you Moab! You have perished, O people of Chemosh!"*[7]

We have no way of knowing how Ruth and Orpah became wives to Mahlon and Chilion, nor can we speculate regarding the religious struggles that took place in their homes as they accommodated and adjusted to such polarised beliefs. It may well have been that, in the providence of God, Ruth softened during the years of her marriage while Orpah merely tolerated the inbuilt differences in hers. However, of one thing we can be absolutely sure: God had a purpose in the grace that was at work in Ruth's heart, a purpose that would cause her to make such a moving confession of faith, and cause Him to move Matthew to write her name in the opening genealogy of his gospel.[8] On the other hand, the absence of conviction in Orpah's life meant the absence of confession, and, when encouraged to go back to the whole upbringing associated with *"her mother's house,"*[9] she turned around for she had no reason to go on!

Only Ruth was affected by what we might call the strangeness of God's grace. Years later, her great grandson, David, went *"to Mizpah of Moab; and he said to the king of Moab, 'Please let my father and mother come here with you, till I know what God will do for me.'"*[10] How sad, that David expected better treatment for his parents in Moab than was likely from King Saul! His wise linkage of Mizpah of Moab with knowing the will of God, helps us to see that he expected even this Mizpah to live up to the meaning of its namesake in Genesis 31:49 where Laban used its watchtower connotation and said, *"May the LORD watch between you and me when we are absent one from another."* He was in no doubt that the One who had been like a watchtower for his great-grandmother would prove Himself as such for him.

Bethlehem

Unlike the Song in our previous chapters, which seemed to change octaves according to the bride's mood, the story of Ruth starts off well and rises to a crescendo, and traces more fully the journey of the church. God often does His greatest works from small beginnings. Had He not done this in creation, when the crowning glory of His work was formed from the dust of the ground, and his bride from a rib in his side? Did Ruth have a small beginning, perhaps while sitting in her little home with her husband and the Spirit of God moved her heart? Or was it that He comforted her as she grieved over his death? Something certainly stirred her to set out on that journey when her mother-in-law, Naomi, heard *"that the LORD had visited His people by giving them bread."*

Yes, Orpah also seemed to have been moved, but her natural response would never be enough. Her earlier resolve *'drooped'* (Heb. *'araph* – the root of her name), and it was as if she drew a line on the road. Moab to Bethlehem was a long walk, thirty miles or so, and it proved long enough for one to think it was too long. For her, it was so far and no farther; but for Ruth it was the point of no return. Orpah couldn't go forward, and Ruth couldn't go back! There was something much deeper going on in her, and then the real beginning was reached. Listen to her outpouring:

> *"Entreat me not to leave you, or to turn back from following after you; for wherever you go, I will go; and wherever you lodge, I will lodge; your people shall be my people, and your God, my God. Where you die, I will die, and there will I be buried. The LORD do so to me, and more also, if anything but death parts you and me." When she saw that she was determined to go with her, she stopped speaking to her."*[11]

Her commitment never wavered and, living up to the background meaning of her name, she was a true *friend* and *companion,* and she completed the journey like a true *neighbour.* She is a real example to us of what we are as believers in our walk with Christ: *"friends,"*[12] *"companion,"*[13] and *"neighbour."*[14] If only we can be all three as faithfully as she was! From then on, her experience was one of continually entering in. She entered into Bethlehem in chapter 1, into the blessings of the field in chapter 2, into a relationship with Boaz in chapter 3, and into the joy of her bridegroom in chapter 4.

Finding grace

By her own admission, Ruth's ambition was not simply to find ears of grain, but eyes of grace.[15] Consistent with her earlier heartfelt confession on the road, she was convinced that finding grace lay in a person and not merely in a place. As God had planned it, her story doesn't focus solely on the progress she made by gleaning, but more so while sitting, walking and standing with her redeemer. In a very distinct way, she points forward to the unlimited blessings outlined for believers in Christ in the epistle to the Ephesians. Meeting Boaz in the field was like our coming to the *"Lord of the harvest,"*[16] which reminds us that we are blessed *"with every spiritual blessing in the heavenly places in Christ."*[17]

No matter whether she was sitting, walking or standing with him, she was like us, as we *"sit ... walk"* and *"stand"*[18] with Christ. Oh, it's so vital that we know where we do sit, and walk, and stand; and equally important that we know where we shouldn't. As Psalm 1:1 teaches so clearly, we don't walk with ungodly advisers, we don't stand shoulder to shoulder with sinners, and we don't sit idly in the company of mockers. Christian, are you sure that where you sit, and with whom you sit, in earthly places reflects where you sit, and with Whom, in the heavenly places?

Like Israel of old, we sit and walk and stand with God. It was through David that God revealed, *"The LORD said to my Lord, 'Sit at My right hand,'"*[19] but it is to New Testament believers that He reveals the great truth that He *"made us sit together in the heavenly places in Christ."*[20] He told His people through Moses, *"I will walk among you and be your God,"*[21] and He has told us, *"I will dwell in them and walk among them."*[22] He also said to Moses, *"Here is a place by Me, and you shall stand upon the rock."*[23] Moses knew what it was to stand on the same rock where God stood.

In a similar way, Amos tells us, *"I saw the LORD standing by the altar."*[24] Most versions say "by" or "beside," but the Hebrew word '*al* means 'over" or "upon," which suggests that Amos had a vision of God standing above the altar in fellowship with its sacrifice, its blood and its flame. Each present-day believer stands in the grace of God,[25] we stand in *"the purpose of God according to election,"*[26] so we also stand on the accepted sacrifice of Christ. So, we sit where God sits, we walk where He walks, and we stand where He stands. For Ruth, the way forward was marked in three ways:

1. By Boaz' **permission**: *"You will listen, my daughter, will you not? Do not go ... but stay close"* (2:8);
2. By Boaz' **protection**: *"Have I not commanded the young men not to touch you?"* (2:9);
3. By Boaz' **provision**: *"And when you are thirsty"* (2:9, 14-16; 3:15-17).

This appeal was for her **acceptance**. Listening meant absorbing two different things: she had to digest his request and the indication of a relationship in the way he greeted her as "my daughter," which can be translated as *"the apple"* of the eye."[27] His appeal was a genuine offer of his **guidance**, and responding meant acknowledging his boundaries and the limitations these set on his permission. This called for her **obedience**. His terms determined where and with whom she would have fellowship: always, and only, in his own field with his own.

His first question shows that her sense of obligation was framed within the expectation of his grace, and his second question was posed in such a way that he wanted her recognition of what he had done. Rather than use a double negative, he could have said, "I have commanded the young men not to touch you," but, for the second time, he put the onus on her by using the word *"not"* twice. By doing this, she understood that his authority applied to his permission and his protection: she was affected by it, and so were they.

His permission and protection also guaranteed his provision in the atmosphere and heat of a dusty field. *"When"* put no limit on how often she went, but he had much more in mind that would satisfy her hunger as well as her thirst. How like the Lord Jesus who has promised, *"He who comes to Me shall never hunger, and he who believes in Me shall never thirst."*[28] We begin to walk with Him by being *"made to drink of one Spirit,"*[29] and we know the sequel to being able to *"draw water from the wells of salvation."*[30] Let's notice how full Boaz' provision was for her and what it supplied.

- It was for her **comfort**, as he invited her to *"Come here, and eat of the bread, and dip your piece of bread in the vinegar."*[31] She was no longer resting alone *"in the house,"*[32] but now felt included;
- It gave her some **company**, as *"she sat beside the reapers."* She was not only close to them, she was close to him, and this is a reminder

of what believers have together for *"truly our fellowship is with the Father and with His Son Jesus Christ"*[33];
- It assured her of his **communion**, as *"he passed parched grain to her; and she ate and was satisfied."* She was within hand's reach of him and, having worked with her own hands in gleaning and dipping, she now enjoyed the work of his hands. *"Parched grain"* meant it had been gathered and prepared by him – roasted by fire. We can learn a valuable lesson here: what we gather ourselves from the Word is good, but what we get direct from the Lord is better. His feeding is the result of the sufferings of the cross, and what comes from that fire will always satisfy.

Please let me glean and gather (2:7, 14; 3:7)

Her measure was limited by the work of her own hands, but there is no indication of how much she actually gathered by herself. By contrast, the measure Boaz gave was unlimited by his heart. Whether in reaching out to his full hand or lying at his feet *"at the end of the heap of grain,"* she entered into his fulness. With his harvest fully gathered, *"his heart was cheerful,"* and he had good reason for it to be so, but so did she for very soon, as his bride, she would enter into the joy of her lord and her redeemer! Little did she know that the Passover that marked her coming to Bethlehem, and the threshing floor that marked her coming to Boaz, would be listed among the Old Testament's God-given symbols of the cross:

- The Passover lamb (Ex.12:1-14);
- The Altar's sacrifice (Lev.1:5);
- The Tree that removes bitterness (Ex.15:25);
- The Threshing floor (2 Chron.3:1);
- The Winepress (Num.18:27, 30);

- The Sword (Zech.13:7).

Then she told her all that the man had done for her (3:16)

Ruth didn't go home to tell Naomi all that she had done for him. No, her whole conversation was about *"the man,"* and that is how it should be for us, too. The problem is, we can be more ready to talk about what we do for the Lord than of what He has done, and is doing, for us. Fascination with *"the Man"* is the answer, but do we have that? By arriving at the beginning of the barley harvest, she made the great discovery that *"As for God, His way is perfect,"*[34] and so is His timing. It is so perfect He knew that Calvary would mark the fulfilment of the Passover, and that a far greater Lord of the harvest would be able to say, *"It is finished!"* This was *"the joy that was set before Him"* as He *"endured the cross"*[35] for He knew this was the only way to bring us to the Passover Lamb, our Redeemer and to our Bridegroom.

Ruth may have wondered at what we have thought of as the strangeness of grace, but in chapter 2:10 she was more concerned about being a stranger. Owning her proper place before Boaz, *"she fell on her face, bowed down to the ground, and said to him ... I am a foreigner (RV, stranger)."* How much more, then, should we be before our Lord and Saviour as we wait to meet Him as our Bridegroom. Boaz gave all that was needed to redeem his bride. He was *"a man of great wealth,"* yet bride-less. He had been near to his people, his workers, and the leaders, but in the end much closer to his bride. As strangers to grace who have been reached and saved, we thank God that our Lord Jesus Christ, *"in whom are hidden all the treasures of wisdom and knowledge,"* gave His all that His bride might be even nearer to Him.

HIS AND MINE

His the grief, and His the glory; (Is.53:3; Lk.24:26)
His the conquest of the hour; (Heb.2:14)
His the shame, and His the splendour; (Matt.27:30; 1 Tim.3:16)
His the weakness and the power. (2 Cor.13:4)
He the Victim and the Victor; (Jn 19:16,30)
He the Sacrifice and Son; (Eph.5:2; Gal.2:20)
He, the Man of matchless wonder, (Matt.8:27 KJV)
Such a victory has won. (1 Cor.15:57)

His the battle of the ages; (Ps.24:8)
His the fight outside the gate; (Heb.13:12)
His the triumph from that hour; (Jn 12:27)
His the grand eternal weight. (Acts 7:55)
He the Bearer of atonement; (2 Cor.5:21)
He the Cleanser of my sin; (Heb.1:3; 9:14)
He, the Man in His enthronement, (Heb.1:8,9)
Risen Conqueror entered in. (Heb.9:24)

Crowned with thorns, and crowned with glory; (Matt.27:29; Heb.2:9)
Suffering Man and Sovereign Lord; (Acts 2:23)
Died to take away my burden; (1 Pet.2:24)
Lives to bring me near to God. (1 Pet.3:18)
His the work and mine the wonder; (Jn 17:4; Lk.9:43)
His the worth and mine the praise; (Rev.5:12)
His the honour, mine the worship, (Rev.4:10,11)
Endless through eternal days. (1 Pet.4:11)

7

A BRIDAL RESEMBLANCE IN THE CHURCHES

"Coming to Him as to a living stone, rejected indeed by men, but chosen by God and precious, you also, as living stones, are being built up a spiritual house, a holy priesthood, to offer up spiritual sacrifices acceptable to God through Jesus Christ" (1 Pet.2:4).

"Now you are the body of Christ, and members individually" (1 Cor.12:27).

"For I am jealous for you with godly jealousy. For I have betrothed you to one husband, that I may present you as a chaste virgin to Christ" (2 Cor.11:2).

We began our walk in the Garden of Eden and found the first foreshadowing of 'A bride through blood' – that is, of the bridegroom – in the second chapter of Genesis. At the close of each day's work in chapter 1, God expressed His satisfaction by announcing, *"It was good,"* but then in chapter 2:18 He suddenly announced, *"It is not good."* This was because He saw the inadequacy of a perfect man not being complemented by a perfect woman as his bride. Of course, He knew in chapter 1:26-31 that He would provide her and this allowed Him to anticipate that His final day's work would be *"very good."* We also see that all this was done in association with the creation of the earth, and it's interesting to note that the theme continues the whole way to the second last chapter of Revelation where the bride is linked with the new heaven and the new earth.[1] Next, we thought about Rebekah as a foreshadowing of 'A bride through the Spirit,' and of Ruth as 'A bride through redemption,' and these can be summarised as depicting:

- Eve with the first man Adam – Christ as **the last Adam;**
- Rebekah with Isaac – Christ as **the Seed;**
- Ruth with Boaz – Christ as **the Redeemer.**

Others would add:

- Zipporah with Moses – Christ as **the Mediator;**
- Elisheba with Aaron – Christ as **the High Priest;**
- Abigail with David – Christ as **the King.**

Warren Wiersbe writes that Moses, "Rejected by his nation, he took a Gentile bride, and is thus a picture of Christ who is today getting a bride from the nations." Others suggest Abigail, since she was described as *"a woman of good understanding and beautiful appearance,"*[2] and therefore is listed among God's beautiful things.

Later, we saw a bridal resemblance in God's relationship with His people, Israel. Now we come to view the practical outcome of this teaching in the epistles as the Spirit of God takes these three aspects and applies them to:

- The **construction** of the **building**, its **structure**, and to seeing its **security and stability**;
- The **coordination** of the **body**, its **stature**, and to seeing its **unity and activity**;
- The **communion** of the **bride**, her **splendour**, and to seeing her **beauty and purity.**

As we pause to explore this, it's worth saying at the outset that it is far more Christ-exalting, and uplifting for us, to enjoy the similarities between *"the church, which is His body"*[3] and the New Testament churches. Much help can be found in seeing the differences, but this rather negative approach might cause us to miss something far more positive. Yes, it's important to understand the differences, and we will think of these in our next chapter, but it's a great pity if we can list them and miss the similarities, especially if we end up elevating the truths connected to the churches and relegate the truth associated with the church. Churches will never be lifeless and aimless, if their distinctives have 'Resemblance to the Bride' at the core! Perhaps, it should also be said that we will fail to nurture the churches if we don't uphold and adorn other doctrines by relating them to the essential nature of the church. And they cannot possibly have life without loving its liveliness.

A RESEMBLANCE TO THE BUILDING: ITS SECURITY AND STABILITY

This part of our subject is vitally important, and this is because the gracious Holy Spirit wants us to know how vital and valuable it is to God. The Lord teaches us through John 16:13,14 that *"the Spirit of truth ... will guide you into all truth ... for He will take of what is Mine and declare it to you."* By His help, then, we need to let the thought of being in *"the church, which is His body"*[4] mean more to us, as we absorb how much it means to Him, to the Holy Spirit, and to God. Jesus' first reference to it is, *"My church,"*[5] and we should love what He says is "Mine"!

If Colossians 1:15-17 teaches that the Creator of creation holds everything physically together, because *"in Him all things consist,"* then v.14, *"In whom we have our redemption through his blood, the forgiveness of sins,"* and v.18, *"and He is the head of the body,"* must indicate that the Redeemer of redemption holds everything spiritually together. Likewise, since Hebrews 1:1-3 teaches that this same glorious Saviour, God's Son, is physically upholding *"all things by the word of His power,"* we ought to show that God has *"spoken to us by His Son"* and, spiritually speaking, He also upholds us by the word of His power. Individually, as Christians, collectively as churches, as in the church, Christ is the Source, the Supplier and Sustainer of our spiritual health and growth.

Salvation through God's sovereignty should bring submission to His sovereignty. As believers, each of us is being *"conformed to the image of His Son"*[6] because of our union with Him, and this should be reflected in our commitment to *"the gospel of His Son."*[7] It should also be seen in our enjoyment of *"the fellowship of his Son,"*[8] but these can only be to the degree that we are living in communion with Him through *"the Spirit of His Son."*[9] The Source, Supplier and Sustainer of our salvation has an eternal claim on His own and, as all three, our service ought to show the lifelong consequences in His own. We glorify our humanity by bowing to His sovereignty, and He glorifies His Deity by enabling us to bow to His sovereignty. Like Job, each of us can say that such thoughts are *"too wonderful for me,"*[10] and our deepest response is not to question or resist, but to worship.

There's no doubt from Peter's opening chapter that he shared Paul's view of the believer's security in Christ, even though they had different ways of expressing it. Paul's comment in Romans 8:1 is, *"There is therefore now no condemnation to those who are in Christ Jesus,"* and Peter's complementary view is that God has *"begotten us again to a living hope through the resurrection of Jesus Christ from the dead."*[11] The believer's eternal security meant a lot to them, and so did the sense of their stability. It is significant that Peter is the one to whom the Lord said, *"on this rock"* – that is, on the certainty that Jesus is the Christ, the Son of the living God – *"I will build my church."*[12]

In Peter's first letter, we see how he applied the analogy of the building to disciples in spiritual service as they experience the privileges of *"coming to Him."*[13] This helps us to see that, although our initial union with Him was based on His invitation, *"Come to Me,"*[14] our continuing communion is based on our continued coming. The Greek word Peter used for *"coming"* is *proserchomenoi*, and it is plural, whereas its associate *erchomenon* used by the Lord in John 6:37, *"him who comes to Me,"* is singular. So *"coming"* to Christ for salvation is once for all, while our *"coming"* in service is on-going. When the Lord went on to say in v.44, *"No one can come to Me unless the Father who sent Me draws him,"* He used *elthein*, which is the aorist tense of the verb, and Peter used the present tense in his letter.

One well-known commentator says, "The compound verb **coming** (*proserchomenoi*), however, conveys more than a mere drawing close to Christ for salvation. The preposition *pros* is a prefix to the normal verb *erchomai* and adds intensity, denoting a drawing near to Christ in intimate, abiding, personal fellowship. The writer to the Hebrews uses this term a number of times to denote a conscious coming into God's presence with the intent to remain.[15] For Peter, the word implied the movement of the entire inner person into the experience of intimate and on-going communion with Christ" (MacArthur Commentary).

Believers are described as *"living stones"* and Christ also is referred to as a *"Living Stone."* He is the *Lithon Zōonta* (singular), we are *lithoi zōontes* (plural), and the image of the building captures the stability and security of our *"in Christ"* relationship. Believers are not simply stones; we are living stones because He has given us life. Without the Builder of the church, we could never experience *"being built up a spiritual house."*[16] We cannot fully enjoy the house-builder unless we enjoy the church-builder! The enjoyment of service must always rest on the enjoyment of salvation, and our enjoyment of teaching must always rest on our enjoyment of the gospel.

A RESEMBLANCE TO THE BODY: IN ITS UNITY AND ACTIVITY

Since Paul was the one who received *"the revelation of the mystery,"*[17] it's no surprise that he wove it so effectively into his epistles. In chapter 12 of Romans, he showed that the transformed life depends on the inseparable link between it and the body. In other words, he was emphasising that it is the gospel of the first eleven chapters that makes possible the practical lifestyle in chapters 12-16. His whole line of reasoning rests on this statement in v.5, *"So we, being many, are one body in Christ,"* and he made a similar case in 1 Corinthians 12:27 – *"Now you are the body of Christ, and members individually."*

He was not implying that believers in Corinth comprised the whole church, which is Christ's body, but rather that the local church was a miniature representation of it and took character from it. In the context of these two chapters, he went on to show how appreciation of body teaching leads on to the application of body teaching through the recognition and interaction of spiritual gifts. These were given at salvation, when He built us into His church; and they function in service: *"For the equipping of the saints for the work of ministry, for the edifying of the body of Christ, till we all come to the unity of the faith and of the knowledge of the Son of God, to a perfect man, to the measure of the stature of the fulness of Christ."*[18]

Paul makes it very clear that fulfilling our God-given roles in the churches depends on what He has fitted us to be as members of His body. He *"has set the members, each one of them, in the body just as He pleased,"*[19] so it's safe to assume that it displeases Him when we don't acknowledge one another as members and recognise each other's gifts. There ought to be body-like coordination in the churches, and it's evident that the divine intention is that our structure should be enhanced by our stature. Paul is an ideal example of one who had a proper view of his brothers and sisters, for he knew how to describe and evaluate them. Listen to him as he thinks of them in different places:

- Rom.16:3 – "My fellow workers in Christ Jesus";
- 1 Cor.1:2 – "To those who are sanctified in Christ Jesus";
- Gal.1:22 – "The churches of Judea which were in Christ";
- Eph.1:1 – "To the saints ... and faithful in Christ Jesus";
- Phil.1:1 – "To all the saints in Christ Jesus";

- Col.1:2 – "To the saints and faithful brethren in Christ";
- 1 Thess.2:14 – "The churches of God which are in Judea in Christ Jesus."

He certainly knew their collective resemblance to the body in its unity and activity, and this should be our aim, too. All these bear their own testimony to what he wrote in 1 Corinthians 10:17, *"For we, though many, are one bread and one body."*

A RESEMBLANCE TO THE BRIDE: IN ITS BEAUTY AND PURITY

Paul's enjoyment of this is as evident as his enjoyment of the building and the body. And it's equally clear that his appreciation of what was made to last and made to live corresponded with his appreciation of what has been made to love. He spent himself on making sure that the churches reflected the church in their construction, the body in their coordination, and now we see the same longing for them to reflect the bride in their communion.

Although he used the phrase, *"that I may present you as a chaste virgin to Christ,"* it never entered his mind that he could add security and stability to the building. Nor did he assume that he could add unity and activity to the body; and it was farthest from his thoughts that he could add beauty and purity to the bride. He was fully aware that he could neither assist nor usurp the role of presenting the church to Him for the work and the joy of presenting the church to Himself, through salvation, is entirely His own. No, his comment in 2 Corinthians 11:2 didn't mean that he thought he could add to the work of Christ, for he had already clarified this earlier in his letter – *"He who raised up the Lord Jesus will also raise us up with Jesus, and will present us with you."*[20] No one knew this better than Paul, and he gave five reasons for this in Ephesians 5:

1. He is Head of the church (v.23);
2. He is the Saviour of the body (v.23);
3. He gave Himself for her (v.25);
4. He might sanctify and cleanse her (v.26);
5. He might present her to Himself (v.27).

The work is all His. Paul's only intention was that all these characteristics would be fulfilled in every local church, and that he would have the joy of seeing them being presentable in their bridal resemblance. But what was he so jealously promoting and guarding? Whatever it was, should we not emulate his desire by encouraging churches to devote themselves to these same high objectives? Let leaders lead, let teachers teach, and let every church live in the atmosphere that Paul longed to see in Corinth by:

- Her bridal faithfulness;
- Her bridal affection;
- Her bridal subjection;
- Her bridal selflessness;
- Her bridal maturity;
- Her bridal compatibility;
- Her bridal purity;
- Her bridal responsibility.

By saying he had *"espoused"* (Gr. *hērmosamēn)* them, he meant that he had taken these features fully into consideration and combined them to make them *"fitted together"* in service for one husband, so that he could fulfil his desire to *"present* (them) *as a chaste virgin to Christ."* But there was a downside. He had a *"fear."* One possibility frightened him, and it was this: he was afraid that their minds could be *"corrupted,"* which means, they would be defiled, spoiled, or withered. In other words, he was terrified that they might lose their bridal resemblance, and this is the worst danger for any Assembly of God's people.

Paul was concerned that sin and failure, whether individually or collectively, could prevent him from his spiritual ambition of *"warning every man and teaching every man in all wisdom, that we may present every man perfect in Christ."*[21] He obviously wouldn't be content with some or many, so he shared this triple focus on *"every man."* Warning, teaching, presenting: this was the apostle's approach, and he knew that fulfilling the third meant having the freedom to fulfil the first two. May we also enjoy the same freedom for *"where the Spirit of the Lord is, there is liberty."*[22] The church, which is His body, faces no such risk of being defiled, spoiled, withered, shrivelled or ruined. The perfect work of Christ has ensured that His promise to *"raise it"* in its entirety, and *"raise him"*[23] individually is guaranteed. Even the adversary himself can't hinder this, but Paul's great ambition to *"present"* each assembly, and each person, *"perfect in Christ"* can be hindered. Satan couldn't undo their salvation, but he could destroy their service, and he can do the same with us. For this reason, our aim also should be to espouse the churches to one husband. It should be our main objective. Until He calls her Home, no one needs his or her assembly to lend a hand in preparing wood, hay or stubble[23] (1 Cor.3:12, RV), but they need all the help they can get to let them see 'a Bridal resemblance in the churches.'

LEAVES & LIVES

"You will be like an oak with fading leaves" (Is.1:30 NIV).

"Therefore we do not lose heart. Even though our outward man is perishing, yet the inward man is being renewed day by day. For our light affliction,

which is but for a moment, is working for us a far more exceeding and eternal weight of glory" (2 Cor.4:16,17 NKJV).

>Leaves that once were raised on high
>Spiral down to reach the ground;
>Fading and discoloured, fly
>In their yellows, reds and browns.
>Each, once full of sap and green,
>With no more to do than die,
>Yet each bud that's left behind
>Says, "New glory will be seen."
>
>Lives that once so ably gave
>Lasting pleasure to the Lord,
>Facing struggles that they have
>With new hardships unexplored.
>Each assured that, like the leaf,
>Even if death comes between,
>Yet His promise in our grief
>Says, "New glory will be seen."
>
>Though the leaf may fade and fall,
>Though the life be in decline,
>Though the outward man decay,
>Let this precious hope define:
>While your spirit is renewed,
>Jesus knows what is unseen,
>And His promise, through His blood,
>Says, "New glory will be seen."

8

SEEING THE DIFFERENCES

"And this I pray, that your love may abound still more and more in knowledge and all discernment, that you may approve the things that are excellent, that you may be sincere and without offense till the day of Christ" (Phil.1:9,10).

As believers in the Lord Jesus Christ, it's important for us to learn how to *"approve the things that are excellent"*[1] or, as some margins put it, "prove the things that differ." In his commentary on Philippians, Albert Barnes says, "The margin here more correctly expresses the sense of the Greek word. The idea is, that he wished them to be able to distinguish between things that are different from each other; to have an intelligent apprehension of what was right and wrong ... He would not have them love and approve all things indiscriminately. They should be esteemed according to their real value. It is remarkable here how anxious the apostle was not only that they should be Christians, but that they should be intelligent Christians, and should understand the real worth and value of objects." How true this is, and how vital that we learn to discriminate the excellence of what

God has revealed.

When it comes to knowing God, we wrestle with the immediate difficulty regarding how the eternal has been made known in time, but also in how the invisible is made visible. In applying this, firstly, to Him, we will be helped in applying much-needed lessons to the wonderful truth of the church, which is Christ's body. Paul's comments in Romans 1:20 give invaluable help, no matter where we live and irrespective of culture or conviction. He could hardly be more definite, as he states, *"For since the creation of the world His invisible attributes are clearly seen, being understood by the things that are made, even His eternal power and godhead, so that they are without excuse."* In other words, God's existence, His Being, character and actions are so evident and comprehensible that it's inexcusable to miss them.

In His goodness, having made Himself known in creation, God also makes Himself known in the Creator, and this is set out for us in the opening chapter of John's Gospel. Now the eternal Himself had come into time and the invisible had become visible for, by sending Him, God allowed the world to see the only One who is *"the image of the invisible God."*[2] Now God's existence, Being, character and actions were made evident and comprehensible in a Person, and sinners *"have no excuse for their sin."*[3]

In a similar way, God has done the same with the invisible church. By an invisible transaction, the Lord Jesus builds every believer into an eternal union with Himself by invisibly baptising each one in the Holy Spirit,[4] who has already done His part by convicting them of their sin and need of a Saviour. Through His invisible work of regeneration, He brings them into the invisible experience of new birth and, having done all this, God then begins the lifelong work of making the invisible visible. By public confession, believers are called to testify that they have become children of God, to confirm this in the visible witness of baptism by immersion in water, and visibly to follow the Lord, so that their individual *"progress may be evident to all"*[5] in the visible service of the local church. In this way, God brings us full circle: the invisible things of God are clearly seen, and the invisible church, in its existence, being, character and actions, is visibly being made known.

Approve

God never intends that we try to apply the Scriptures without first approving them. It's not that He is looking for our approval, but that we should test our reasoning; otherwise, we will not discern what He wants us to understand. He wants us to *"approve"* it, and His Word helps us to do this by showing how He intends us to interpret the word Paul used. In 1 Corinthians 11:28, he draws from the same word and urges us to *"examine"* ourselves before participating in remembering Him by eating the bread and drinking the cup.

Peter also uses a related word when he speaks of gold being *"tried"* by fire. Some English versions have attempted to clarify the implications by translating Luke 12:56 (ASV, NASB) by saying, how to *"interpret"* or how to *"analyze."* Take a gold-miner, for example: he sets out to recognise the properties of real gold, and these form his benchmark for dismissing pyrite (fool's gold) and other minerals of lesser value. While panning, he may build his hopes on whatever gleams among the ore, convincing himself that he has 'struck gold,' only to have his hopes dashed by someone who knows more about its properties than he does. For this reason, the Assay Office is his friend, even though he may leave it disappointed that his supposed nugget isn't real gold after all. Similarly, students of God's Word are rewarded through the careful examination and analysis of their beliefs and conclusions. Over the centuries, this has been the downfall of many who have built upon non-biblical beliefs, while claiming them to be nuggets of truth.

Scripture gives its own safeguard to this, and Acts 17:11 outlines in detail how we can avoid such error: *"These were more fair-minded than those in Thessalonica, in that they received the word with all readiness, and searched the Scriptures daily to find out whether these things were so."* Our own day is no different from Paul's, since he found that people react differently when truth is taught. He and Silas discovered in Thessalonica that people were divided when they *"reasoned with them from the Scriptures,"* yet there was a different response when they moved on to Berea.

First of all, they were *"more fair-minded,"* in that they were good listeners and good learners. Secondly, they *"received the word,"* accepting it and submitting to it. Thirdly, they did this *"with all readiness of mind,"* that is without hesitation and with forward thinking. They realised that submitting to the mind of God doesn't make believers mindless. Fourthly, they did this daily, not spasmodically. Fifthly, they *"searched the Scriptures,"* which means they examined what they read; applying questions to the Word and to themselves as they investigated what it teaches. These five points are an essential guide to sound Bible study, so it helps if we ask ourselves five fairly incisive questions:

1. Am I fair-minded, in that I truly want to listen and learn?
2. Am I accepting what God teaches and submitting to it?
3. Am I doing this without hesitation and with a forward-thinking attitude?
4. Am I spending time in the Word every day?
5. Am I a searcher who enjoys the exploration and explanation of what God is saying?

The banker lives by a similar principle: learning the resemblances of each denomination of currency allows differences to be found, rather than making a study of endless counterfeits. But God doesn't intend that we relate to what He reveals merely by seeing how it differs from something else He has shown, and this is paramount if we are to enjoy applying the wonderful truth of the church to the churches. It is far from being enough, if all we can see are the differences.

Excellent

The word *"excellent"* comes from the Greek word *diapherō*, which literally means to carry through, and this is the meaning Mark gave to it when the Lord spoke about those who brought wares to carry through the Temple in Mark 11:16. Paul applies it to what we carry through in our reasoning, and this is not only important, it is vital. It's much better to be in the Temple to carry through what is of God and for God; and much better to be mining for the treasure of real gold with a discerning eye that isn't taken in by all that glitters.

Our aim is very similar: a clear understanding and heartfelt enjoyment of the church, which is His body will ensure that we delight in the resemblances to His church in the churches, and not be content simply to describe the differences. Yes, there are distinctions – God-given distinctions – but He wants us to see these in the context of reflecting and enjoying the connections. We may put it like this: the gold-miner is not a whit better off by listing the differences between the worthless ore in his hand and the glint of the real thing; and the banker is no better off by hoarding what looks real, but isn't. Be that as it may, to be among what Mr Barnes has called "Intelligent Christians" we must focus on the Christ-exalting opportunity of the nature of the churches being church-based, and the nurture of the churches being church-based.

This will safeguard what we *"approve."* It also will help us to be satisfied by what is *"excellent,"* and enable the resemblances and differences to go hand-in-hand. In His goodness, God has given us three avenues to the resources we have in His Word, and we can draw from them as we devote ourselves to:

His Headship

Our Spiritual feeding is, first of all, utterly dependent on belonging to Christ. He has said, *"Without Me you can do nothing"*[6] and this applies to our growing as much as it does to our doing! The secret lies in *"holding fast to the Head, from whom all the body, nourished and knit together by joints and ligaments, grows with the increase that is from God."*[7] If we have never done it before, we need to take the questions we borrowed from the Bereans and ask, "Am I fulfilling each of these with Him?" Is my mind fixed on Him? Am I accepting and submitting to what I learn from him? Do I spend time daily with Him? If I want to say, *"He must increase, but I must decrease,"*[8] then this *"must"* has to mean that my growth comes from *"holding fast to the Head."* He has said, *"Take My yoke upon you and learn of Me,"*[9] and He should be my first reason and first resource for learning.

Discipleship

Alongside the Lord as our Teacher, He also has taught us to *"make disciples ... teaching them to observe all things that I have commanded you,"*[10] so part of our discipleship is that others teach us. Paul and Barnabas are real examples of this. When they went to Derbe, *"they preached the gospel ... and made disciples,"* then they moved on to other cities: *"strengthening the souls of the disciples, exhorting them to continue in the faith."*[11] They were teachers modelled on the Teacher, and this is what disciples need us to be toward them.

Stewardship

A vital part of our calling is that we commit ourselves as *"servants of Christ and stewards of the mysteries of God. Moreover it is required in stewards that one be found faithful."*[12] By combining these two ministries, Christ-ward and man-ward, Paul indicates that the mind of the servant – in this case, based on *hupēretēs*, as an under-oarsman of Christ – is the ideal mind-set of the steward who is expected to manage or oversee the presentation of things formerly understood until they were revealed by God. What an honour to get close to others as stewards by, first of all, being close enough to Christ as His servants!

Before concluding his first letter to Corinth, Paul urged the church to see *"a more excellent way."* In chapter 11:28, he had encouraged them to *"examine"* themselves for holiness. In chapter 12 he urged them to have unity; and in chapter 13, he directed them to love. In spite of all their differences, he wanted them to adopt the resemblances, so that *"in Corinth"*[13] they might be seen as being *"in Christ"*!

Study it carefully,
Think of it prayerfully,
Deep in thy heart let its pure precepts dwell.
Slight not its history,
Ponder its mystery,
None can e'er prize it too fondly or well.
(Author unknown)

Twelve Differences

1. **THE CHURCH** - Includes all Christians at salvation through baptism in the Spirit (Acts 1:5; 1 Cor.12:13)/ **THE CHURCHES** - Those who are saved, baptised by immersion in water, and added (Acts 2:41; 8:35-38; 18:8);
2. **THE CHURCH** - One church from Pentecost to the Rapture: "So we, being many, are one body in Christ, and individually members one of another " (Rom.12:5). "There is one body"(Eph.4:4)/ **THE CHURCHES** - Many churches – Acts 9:31. Judea, Samaria, Galilee (2 Cor.8:1, Macedonia (Gal.1:2,22), Galatia (1 Pet.1:1) - Asia;
3. **THE CHURCH** - Saints, members, sheep, neither male nor female (Rom.1:7; 12:5; Jn 10:26-28; Gal.3:28)/ **THE CHURCHES** - Disciples, man, woman, brothers, sisters (1 Cor.11:11; 1 Cor.7:15; Col.3:18);
4. **THE CHURCH** - Can't be lost from it (Jn 6:39; 17:12; 18:9)/ **THE CHURCHES** - Can leave or be removed (1 Cor.5:13; 2 Tim.1:15);
5. **THE CHURCH** - Christ is the Builder (Matt.16:18)/ **THE CHURCHES** - Planted by men (1 Cor.3:6-9,12);
6. **THE CHURCH** - Still belong to it after death (Rom.8:38; 2 Cor.5:8; 1 Thess.4:16; 2 Tim.1:12)/ **THE CHURCHES** - Cease to belong at death (1 Cor.15:20);
7. **THE CHURCH** - Christ as Head and Shepherd (Eph.1:22; 4:15; 5:23; Col.1:18; 2:10,19)/ **THE CHURCHES** - Elders rule and shepherd (Acts 14:23; 20:28; 1 Pet.5:2);
8. **THE CHURCH** - Indivisible (Jn 6:37; 18:9; Eph.5:27)/ **THE CHURCHES** - Can suffer splits (Acts 8:1; Gal.1:13);
9. **THE CHURCH** - Eternal and inviolable: "The gates of Hades shall not prevail against it" (Matt.16:18)/ **THE CHURCHES** - Temporal – can cease, be damaged and destroyed (Rev.2:5; 3:16; 1 Cor.3:17; Acts 8:1; Gal.1:13);
10. **THE CHURCH** – Universal (1 Cor.12:13; Gal.3:28)/ **THE CHURCHES**

SEEING THE BRIDE IN ALL THE SCRIPTURES

– Local 1 Cor.1:2; Rev.1:4);
11. **THE CHURCH** - No false members (Jn 3:36; Eph.2:8)/ **THE CHURCHES** - Can have false people, teachers (Matt.7:16; Jude 4,12,13,19; Acts 20:29);
12. **THE CHURCH** - Made perfect (Heb.10:14)/ **THE CHURCHES** - Being perfected (2 Cor.7:1; 11:2,3; Gal.3:3; Col.1:28, see also 2 Cor.11:2,3).

SEEING YOU – SEEING HIM

God's Word is sure, He settled it in heaven, (Ps.119:89)
Though here on earth it may not seem to be.
Debates and lives still linger on unsettled,
With minds storm-tossed, just like the troubled sea.

Unsure on earth? Yes, reason here is earthly,
Our thoughts and ways are nothing like His own; (Is.55:8,9)
But these will be transformed when what is heavenly
Transcends nature, and godly we become. (1 Cor.2:14)

Unstable here, established in the heavens:
The contrast says there's no foundation near.
God is the source of inspired revelation, (2 Tim.3:16)
Not man, who lives in this ungodly sphere.

God's monumental Word will stand forever, (Is.40:8)
Because, like God, it dwells in heaven above.
Its basis, truths, and promise failing never
For each is sure within eternal love.

But let this Word now dwell within us richly, (Col.3:16)
Then what is sure in heaven is sure in us;
Our doubts and fears will disappear, and swiftly

SEEING THE DIFFERENCES

Our hearts are shaped by His *"word of the cross."* (1 Cor.1:18)

Feed on it daily. It's necessary for you. (Prov.30:8)
Don't scan or skim, take time to take it in;
Always dwell deep within its sacred pages,
And He will see your heart is kept from sin. (Ps.119:11)

Not just with pickings from your own past gleanings
Or from a sheaf you reaped along the way,
But that your own approach to daily readings
Will let you see the Saviour in your day.

9

SUFFERING OR REJOICING

"But God composed the body, having given greater honour to that part which lacks it, that there should be no schism in the body, but that the members should have the same care for one another. And if one member suffers, all the members suffer with it; or if one member is honoured, all the members rejoice with it. Now you are the body of Christ, and members individually" (1 Cor.12:25-27).

Many of these differences between the church and the churches are biblically supported. We can be justifiably thankful for the comparisons and contrasts we see, that make us rejoice in the security of our salvation with its eternal hope by being "in Christ." These are of legitimate spiritual significance for our obedience to the lordship of Christ in our daily walk with Him. For instance, none of us needs to be baptised by immersion in water to be in the church, which is His body, *"for in one Spirit were we all baptized into one body,"*[1] and Jesus Himself is the Baptizer.[2]

The danger comes when we find differences that have no support in

Scripture. Because of this, God invites us through Paul to consider differences that prevent us from resembling the harmony of *"the body."* He reminds us that God has "composed" the body, by which he means it is combined and blended in such a way that there are no divisions in it. Sadly, in the previous chapter, he said to the church in Corinth, *"I hear that there are divisions among you,"*[3] and this was only part of their wider problem. Paul, rightfully, had concerns about its state:

- Divisions and contentions (ch.1-3);
- Judging each other (ch.4);
- Immorality (ch.5);
- Lawsuits between brethren (ch.6);
- Marriage problems (ch.7);
- Stumbling over eating habits (ch.8);
- Questioning apostleship (ch.9);
- Wrong behaviour at the Remembrance (chs.10-11);
- Problems over spiritual gifts (chs.12-14);
- Questioning the gospel – for example, the resurrection of believers (ch.15).

There's not one chapter that doesn't refer to a problem in that church. We could describe it as a hotbed of trouble. What a contrast, then, that there is *"no schism in the body"*: no divisions, no splits, and no gaps between its members! To emphasis his point, the word "schism" is singular, which means there's not even one example of division. It sounds like an exceptionally high standard, and unlikely that we could ever resemble "the body." But is it beyond us? No, at the beginning of Acts 2, the believers were described as being *"with one accord in one place"* – homou epi to auto – which literally means 'together together' or 'together upon the one thing.' Their togetherness was explicitly in one place for one purpose, and was a wonderful display of the unity they enjoyed under the outpouring of the Holy Spirit.

At the end of Acts 2, this was seen in the gathering of newly converted, baptised and added disciples who formed the first church in Jerusalem. Verse 44 says, *"Now all who believed were together"* in close fellowship, and as a lovely reflection of "the body" that God still wants all the churches to resemble. These two Spirit-led gatherings began on the Day of Pentecost: the church, which is His body, and the first of the local churches that we find in The Acts and throughout the New Testament. As *"they continued steadfastly in the apostles' doctrine and fellowship, in the breaking of bread, and in prayers,"*[4] everyone showed that they would:

- **Assent** – consistent **agreement** with the Lord's teaching;
- **Attend** – consistent **commitment** to assembly gatherings;
- **Adhere** – consistent **fulfilment** of daily testimony.

In this way, they showed how much they cared for what the Lord had done for them in calling them into His church and, at the same time, to serve Him in the local church. No wonder *"they continued steadfastly"*! And we may well ask, "How could anyone ever continue haphazardly?" But that wasn't all: within their fellowship there was a real sense of fellow-interest and fellow-feeling for they *"had all things in common,"*[5] in that they also cared for one another. They were a good working example of church service being inclusive, and showed that fellowship is never exclusive.

The same care for one another

God never intended that we should ever attempt to have minds fixed on His purpose without having thoughtfulness for His people. It sounds like another tall order in a world of social structures, class distinction and casteism. In the wonder of the church, which is His body, Christ as the Builder has the same regard for each living stone; as Baptizer, He has the same desire for each member; and, as the Bridegroom, He has the same love for every believer. In the local church, we should see each other as we are "in Christ," making no distinction between rich and poor, well-educated and uneducated, favouring some because of their evident spiritual gifts while overlooking others who seem less gifted. In other words, there is no room in a church for partiality and prejudice. God has no place for a caring–uncaring admixture. He wants to see *"the same care"* being available to all, irrespective of their circumstances.

All the members suffer with it

No matter where a body suffers, the whole body feels it. This is true physically. Tears flow when a foot hurts, yet the foot is nowhere near the eyes. There are many ways in which a church can prove that supported hurt is never isolated. The heart of God showed this when His people were assured that *"In all their affliction He was afflicted."*[6] In their distresses, He was distressed; in their anguish, He felt anguish. Likewise, the Lord Jesus Christ shed silent tears over the death of Lazarus,[7] yet calmed a tearful widow on the way to bury her son.[8] When the heart of a local assembly is affected by someone's hurt, as an example of *"the Christ,"* it reflects the heart of Christ and feels as He feels. Sorrows in a local church can run very deeply, and the fellow feeling of true sympathy surrounds the sorrowing, causing them to know that, *"The Lord is with them that uphold my soul."*[9]

All the members rejoice with it

This is the other side of the same coin. Churches that feel the pains of others are more likely to share their joys. Be those of a personal, family or a church nature, tender hearts are best at rejoicing. A dear elderly sister was troubled about someone who refused to speak to her, because of some unintended offence. What should she do? Having suggested she contact the person and read Ephesians 4:32, it was no surprise that its message to *"be kind to one another, tender-hearted, forgiving one another, even as God in Christ forgave you"* put everything right. God did it for us *"in Christ"* and we should do it for one another, since we are in *"the Christ"*!

Members of Christ's body may be honoured and complimented for the help their gift brings to others, and the main reason for giving praise is that they are imparting what Christ, as Head, is providing. Reluctance to rejoice with the person may well be a reluctance to acknowledge that *"God has set the members, each one of them, in the body just as He pleased,"*[10] and that we also should be pleased. But rejoicing is not an empty outburst of flattering congratulations; it is best expressed with a real sense of spiritual appreciation and encouragement for the fulfilment of their ministry. Paul did this throughout Romans 16, by acknowledging how God had used a number of women, plus men, to fulfil their God-given roles. While writing to another church as a whole, he was not averse to giving a word of personal encouragement: "And say to Archippus, *'Take heed to the ministry which you have received in the Lord, that you may fulfill it.'"*[11] And, writing personally to young Timothy, he urged him, *"Do not neglect the gift that is in you ... that your progress may be evident to all."*[12]

The danger is, that those who are negligent may never discover or develop their own gift and, by showing neither aptitude nor ability, may respond with rivalry rather than rejoicing when someone else makes progress. The intended response is that they keep being united in joy to show how real their unchanging share is in the other person's thankfulness, satisfaction and fulfilment. Paul is very straightforward and adopts three lines of reasoning, and it's easy for us to see how he applies them. Bearing this in mind, we can follow Paul's thoughts on how the church has only three aspects to its combined witness.

1. **Analogy**: The analogy of the various members in the human body spontaneously interacting for each other's welfare (1 Cor.12:12-17);
2. **Theology**: The spiritual concept of all the members of the church, which is His body, being in complete harmony together (1 Cor.12:18-26);
3. **Application**: The expected application of this character and conduct in each local assembly's service and fellowship (1 Cor.12:27).

1. Made known through local churches

His application is totally in keeping with his earlier comment in v.25 where he speaks about how we should see each other in Christ, before moving on to show how we should treat each other. By doing this, he emphasises that the individual Christian and the local church gatherings are called to be consistent with body teaching. He also impresses this great truth in Romans 12:5 by saying to the church in Rome, *"so we, being many, are one body in Christ, and individually members of one another."* Individually, we should uphold the character of the *"member"* in everything we say and do; and collectively, the local church should uphold the character of *"the body of Christ."*[13] This doesn't mean that each church is the body of Christ, otherwise we would have to conclude that there are multiple bodies. Paul didn't include the definite article, so he really said, *"You are body of Christ"* to stress the importance of churches representing and resembling the unity that is seen in the harmony and holiness of His church.

This is exceptionally special for it means that the divine concept of a local church, and of each brother and sister in it, is modelled on something far grander. It also means that churches in their localities, in spite of limitations and failings, including struggles with the flesh that sometimes reveal inter-personal difficulties, are called to resemble a building, a body, and a bride. Every church is made up of individuals whose calling is *"high,"*[14] *"holy,"*[15] and *"heavenly,"*[16] and this lofty desire from the heart of an eternal God should find the willing response that is voiced by each one of us and by all the churches, *"Therefore we make it our aim ... to be well pleasing to Him."*[17]

2. Made known through members coupled in marriage

God made it clear in the first book of the Old Testament that Adam was *"joined to his wife"* in their marital bond. The Lord Jesus quoted this in the first book of the New Testament, and immediately added, *"Therefore what God has joined together, let not man separate."*[18] Across centuries and cultures, the will of God remained, and remains, unchanged, because the bridal image of "the church" has the second aspect of its witness presented in the marriages of born-again believers. We know that marriage in general is not the witness, but of those who are *"members of His body."*[19] It's identical reasoning to what was applied to the church in Rome in its witness, because they were *"members of one another."* Paul has given us a delightful likeness to Christ and His church in Ephesians 5:22-33, by lifting up the image of a husband-wife relationship.

The resemblance is so strong, that, in the scope of these twelve verses,

Paul mentions the *"church"* and the *"body"* eight times. Before concluding his reasoning, he very significantly brings Genesis 2 and Matthew 19 right up to date by saying, *"For this reason a man shall leave his father and mother and be joined to his wife, and the two shall become one flesh."* The intended witness is very important. Having called churches to *"make all see"*[20] the great truth of Christ and His church, so Christian married couples in their closest bond as members of His body should cause others to see something so special in their marriage. As churches, and as couples, we ask if we do.

3. Made known to the principalities and powers

This third aspect of witness lifts us into a higher dimension altogether! The previous two have focused on earth-bound churches and couples in their small representations of the church, but the third focuses on its witness in heavenly places through the entire church. It's such an extraordinary revelation that God's intent is *"that now the manifold wisdom of God might be made known by the church to the principalities and powers in the heavenly places."* But, which principalities and powers does Paul mean? Are they the *"innumerable company"* of Hebrews 12:22 or those against whom believers wrestle in Ephesians 6:12? Are they the host who are *"holy ... His ... elect"*[21] or those who fell with the devil?[22]

Without doubt, both are affected by the triumph of the cross and by the blood-bought security of the redeemed. We know from Revelation 5:12 that those who gather around the throne in heaven *"desire to look into"*[23] our great salvation, and cry, *"Worthy is the Lamb who was slain to receive power and riches and wisdom, and strength and honour and glory and blessing!"* So they rejoice in seeing the many facets of God's wisdom.

What then of those fallen angels? Why would there be a witness of the church to them? Perhaps, firstly, as a reinforcing of their leader's defeat at the cross where the Saviour went *"that through death He might destroy him who had the power of death, that is, the devil."*[24] Two thousand years later, we are still in the *"now"* of God's intent to proclaim His *"manifold wisdom ... by the church,"* that, as Christ was unconquerable, so also is *"the church."* No matter how much these forces attack believers who need the armour of God for protection, they cannot reach beyond our Protector. As Christ, so also is the eternal security of *"the Christ"*: in Him, we are unreachable and unconquerable.

MAN'S PLAN – GOD'S PURPOSE

They dragged the precious Christ to Calvary, (Lk.22:54)
Though He had only, ever come to draw; (Jn 12:32)
They hated Him whose very name is Love,
And for their sake came to fulfil the Law. (Is.42:21)

They broke the self-same Law He came to keep
And cast aside the One His Father gave; (Is.53:3; Jn 3:16)
They put to death the One who makes men live; (Acts 3:15)
And lost the Paschal Lamb who came to save. (Jn 1:29)

With brutal force the meek and gentle One, (2 Cor.10:1)
Though guiltless was condemned by guilty men (1 Pet.1:19)
Whose ire defied the Prince of Peace, God's Son, (Is.9:6)
Who rose unhindered to His throne again.

They could not break His legs, yet pierced His side, (Jn 19:33,34)
According to God's own prophetic Word. (Acts 4:27,28)
They could not hinder these truths being applied,
Nor could their spear disable His great sword. (Zech.13:7)

They could discard the sign, but not the King; (Jn 19:19)
They could remove the cross, but not the Name;
Nor could they stop the sons that He would bring (Heb.2:10)
To glory, in fulfilment of His aim.

Their mocking taunts fell silent long ago;
And those who shouted, they are fallen, too, (Ps.2:1-5)
But heaven's exalted King wants us to know (Ps.2:6)
His bride will rise from Gentile and the Jew. (Eph.2:14)

10

A GLORIOUS CHURCH

"That He might present her to Himself a glorious church, not having spot or wrinkle or any such thing, but that she should be holy and without blemish" (Eph.5:27).

Here is the highest distinction that will ever be conferred on the church: the One who gave Himself for us will give us to Himself! Having already described her as *"My church,"* *"His body"* and *"the Christ,"* He will raise all the members He stood by on earth to stand beside Him in heaven. At the moment of His return, the One who once said His own work on earth for us was finished will say that our work on earth for Him is finished. Heaven will be opened, and we will be ushered into *"the presence of His glory with exceeding joy."*[1] The wonder is, we will not feel out of place.

Will there be elation in heaven? Scripture certainly helps us to see how heaven was moved in its response to creation, *"When the morning stars sang together, and all the sons of God shouted for joy."*[2] When the Saviour left His glorious throne, the angelic host responded to His incarnation.

As one of their number announced His birth, well known language was used to introduce Him as Saviour, Christ and Lord, but then came the uttering of a word that had never been used before: *"Babe."* At that moment, all heaven was moved. *'Suddenly there was with the angel a multitude of the heavenly host praising God and saying, "Glory to God in the highest, and on earth peace, good will toward men!"'*³

Luke is the one who also tells us that, as the Lord entered Jerusalem for His final few days before the cross, *'the whole multitude of the disciples began to rejoice and praise God with a loud voice for all the mighty works they had seen, saying, "Blessed is the King who comes in the name of the LORD!"* It was then they immediately anticipated *"Peace in heaven and glory in the highest."* They were in no doubt that heaven would be moved, and it was as if the angelic message of peace on earth at His birth found its response in disciples' message of peace in heaven. Were they claiming Psalm 148:1,2? *"Praise the LORD! Praise the LORD from the heavens; Praise Him in the heights! Praise Him, all His angels; Praise Him, all His Hosts!"*

We can only assume what heaven was like during the six hours of the cross: firstly, as men abused Him; and then, as God *"laid on Him the iniquity of us all."* Was there silence? Or did the seraphim continued to cry, *"Holy, holy, holy is the LORD of hosts, the whole earth is full of His glory!"*

Then came the triumphant Saviour's resurrection and ascension with another corresponding response in heaven to what had been heard on earth. Luke 1:46-55 has been described as His mother Mary's magnificat for His incarnation, and we could view Hebrews 1:5-14 as His Father's magnificat in His ascension. In the midst of that wonderful exaltation of His Son, the Father says, *"Your throne, O God, is forever and ever; a sceptre of righteousness is the sceptre of Your kingdom. You have loved righteousness* and hated lawlessness; therefore God, Your God, has anointed You with the oil of gladness more than Your companions."

We can almost imagine the whole angelic host standing in awe as the Lord of glory entered in, still bearing the wound-prints of Calvary, and borrow Psalm 24's language to capture the grandeur of His arrival home from the greatest battle of all: *"Lift up your heads, O you gates! And be lifted up, you everlasting doors! And the King of glory shall come in. Who is this King of glory? The Lord strong and mighty, the Lord mighty in battle. Lift up your heads, O you gates! Lift up, you everlasting doors! And the King of glory shall come in. Who is this King of glory? The Lord of hosts, He is the King of glory. Selah."*

If David by divine inspiration could revel in the return of the ark of the covenant, as it prefigured the glorified Christ in the Most Holy Place, then surely the gladness of the Inspirer moved the whole angelic host to rejoice with Him as His Son came back to where He rightly belongs! Think, then, of this: if they were so affected by the homecoming of the Redeemer, what will it be like when He returns home next time with the redeemed as His bride at His side? If *"there is joy in the presence of the angels of God over one sinner who repents,"*[4] what will be their rejoicing at the sight of the whole church arriving with Him as its escort? They had witnessed the loss of Satan and his angels *"who did not keep their proper domain, but left their own abode"*[5] and saw them *"cast down to hell and delivered into chains of darkness, to be reserved for judgment."*[6] Now they wait to see the gain that is coming when heaven will be repopulated by His church.

A glorious church

It's not just a church, it's a *"glorious church,"* but how did it qualify to possess such a name? First of all, it is because our salvation is entirely a work of God. From its beginning, it was designed and utterly dependent on the everlasting purpose of the God of glory,[7] and it came to us by revelation from the Father of glory of whom Paul wrote:

> *"that the God of our Lord Jesus Christ, the Father of glory, may give to you the spirit of wisdom and revelation in the knowledge of Him, the eyes of your understanding being enlightened; that you may know what is the hope of His calling, what are the riches of the glory of His inheritance in the saints, and what is the exceeding greatness of His power toward us who believe, according to the working of His mighty power which He worked in Christ when He raised Him from the dead and seated Him at His right hand in the heavenly places, far above all principality and power and might and dominion, and every name that is named, not only in this age but also in that which is to come. And He put all things under His feet, and gave Him to be head over all things to the church, which is His body, the fullness of Him who fills all in all."*[8]

It is based wholly on the finished work of the Lord of glory[9] *"who was delivered up because of our offences, and was raised for our justification;"*[10] and is ours through the convicting and sanctifying work of the Spirit of glory.[11] They share co-equal glory, having identical attributes, and have worked together to bring every believer *"into the glorious liberty of the children of God."*[12]

The glorious gospel

God always does what He is. In creation, *"The heavens declare the glory of God,"*[13] and, in redemption, the conquest of the Passover lamb led on to a liberating exodus that caused the people to *"sing to the LORD, for He has triumphed gloriously."*[14] In the scope of Exodus 15 God wove the glorious nature of His being and of His working, which we can trace as follows.

*His Name

In verse 3, they sang, *"The LORD is His name,"* and Moses spoke to them about God's *"glorious and awesome name"* in Deuteronomy 28:58. By drawing from the word *kabōd*, he caused the people to think of a name that is weighty, and he linked it to the "awesome" name that is worthy of reverence. However, instead of using both words in their form as nouns, he used verbs to show that this was a name that had to be weighed and revered by them. In other words, they were to learn to experience the name. Moses learned the value of the name for himself when he asked at the burning bush, *"What is His name?"* and the answer came, *"I AM WHO I AM."*[15] How blessed we are, if we adore the deity, identity, and authority of that Name! And how good it is, if God says to us, as He did to Israel, *"Therefore My people shall know My name,"*[16] and we learn it by personal experience.

*His power

In verse 6, they also sang of the Lord's right hand being *"glorious in power,"* and how necessary and valuable His power is in overthrowing the enemy. Coming from the word *adar*, they were being introduced to God's greatness and magnificence, which they saw against the

Egyptians. We also discover it in our warfare against the evil one, therefore we need to be *"strengthened with all might, according to His glorious power."*[17]

*His holiness

In verse 11, their thoughts turned to the incomparable One who is *"glorious in holiness,"* and so we begin to see the cumulative effect of their glorious God, and ours. Now we can consider the glorious holiness of Him with the glorious name; and not only so, but that His glorious name and holiness make Him glorious in power. In the frailty of our minds, we may pray for spiritual power to resist sin and to overcome, when really we should be praying for holiness. Once again, the word is *adar* and it's the magnificence of His holiness that is before us. This is what God is. It's not that He is holy because of the absence of sin, He is sinless because of the presence of holiness. Holiness doesn't describe Him; it defines Him!

It is only in God's goodness to us that the writer of Hebrews 3:1 could call believers *"holy brethren,"* and this rests entirely on what he later says in chapter 10:14, *"For by one offering He has perfected forever those who are being sanctified."* It's through the work of the cross and *"according to His mercy He saved us, through the washing of regeneration and renewing of the Holy Spirit"*[18] that every believer is perfect in Christ. It is Their work, and They will never undo it. The adversary didn't do it; therefore he can never undo it. We didn't do it for ourselves, and neither can we undo it!

His arm

In verse 16, a grateful people sang of their deliverance through the *"arm"* of their Deliverer. Jeremiah says, *"Their Redeemer is strong,"*[19] and He doesn't buy for someone else to steal, or free for someone else to bind. When Isaiah reflected on Moses and the people's redemption and escape from Egypt, He says that God led them *"With His glorious arm."*[20] Yes, redemption is a glorious work performed by a glorious Person, yet Isaiah's question still rings true. *"Who has believed our report? And to whom has the arm of the LORD been revealed?"*[21] Isaiah 53 is God's great declaration that *"the arm of the LORD"* has been revealed in the Person of His Son, the Servant, the Sacrifice, and Saviour. In chapter 63:12, Isaiah speaks of *"His glorious arm"*, and so can we!

> He hath made bare His arm,
> Who shall His work withstand?
> 'Tis He His people's cause defends,
> Who then shall stay His hand?
> (J. Wesley from Paul Gerhardt)

His voice

With their song ended, God made a promise to His people in verse 26, based on one condition: *"If you diligently heed the voice of the LORD your God and do what is right in his sight."* Isaiah speaks of *"His glorious voice,"*[22] using the word *hōd* which refers to its imposing grandeur. No other voice can compare with it, and none should ever compete! The voice of the LORD is powerful, not only because He is mighty for He also speaks in His holiness.[23] Brother and sister, if you want power in prayer, let your voice speak in holiness. If you want power in your preaching, speak in your holiness for then you truly will have power.

He has spoken to us through *"the glorious gospel of the blessed God,"*[24] which can be translated as 'the gospel of the happy God.' We sometimes hear the statement being made that happiness depends on happenings. No, not so: God has happiness in the gospel, because it reveals His glorious name, changes lives by His glorious power, conquers sin by His glorious holiness, brings deliverance by His glorious arm, and speaks to our hearts by His glorious voice. What a gospel! It makes God happy, and those who trust in Christ as their Saviour are made happy too.

The glorious appearing

In keeping with God's happiness in the gospel, Paul says, we are *"looking for the blessed hope"*[25] and, once again, the thought is that we are looking forward expectantly for the happy hope. Only two verses earlier, Paul described the first epiphany of Christ when He came as *"the grace of God that brings salvation has appeared to all men."* It was this appearing that fully secured redemption's foundation and brings repentant sinners into the happiness of the gospel. What a glorious foundation! And it causes each born again believer to rejoice in God, *"who has saved us and called us with a holy calling, not according to our works, but according to His own purpose and grace which was given to us in Christ Jesus before time began."*

It also was because of this *"appearing of our Saviour"* that Paul assured young Timothy *"He brought life and immortality to light through the gospel."*[26] Our word 'epiphany' comes from a Greek word that means to shine and give light, so we are being reminded that Jesus' appearing shines into our lives in the purpose of His first epiphany and by the promise of the second. In speaking to us about the Lord Jesus' next epiphany, he stirs our anticipation even more by calling it our *"blessed hope,"* so that we have the happiness of the gospel behind us, and the happiness of this hope before us of being at home with Him. With Paul, we say that He is *"our great God and Saviour Jesus Christ, who gave Himself for us."*[27]

His glorious body

As all Old Testament prophecy pointed forward to God's greater purpose being fulfilled in the gospel of his Son, it in turn points forward to the greatest promise being fulfilled when He comes for His church. Bearing the purpose in mind, that our Saviour *"brought life and immortality to light through the gospel,"* this will be fully endorsed when, *"The Lord Himself will descend from heaven with a shout, with the voice of an archangel, and with the trumpet of God. And the dead in Christ will rise first. Then we who are alive and remain shall be caught up together with them in the clouds to meet the Lord in the air. And thus we shall always be with the Lord."*[28]

He will not leave any promise unfulfilled, and the One who was known on earth *"for all the glorious things that were done by Him,"*[29] will perform, *"in a moment,"* the greatest mass miracle of all. *"For the trumpet will sound, and the dead will be raised incorruptible, and we shall be changed. For this corruptible must put on incorruption, and this mortal must put on immortality."*[30] Believers who have died, ever since the Day of Pentecost, will be raised in fulfilment of the Lord's promise, *"I am the resurrection and the life. He who believes in Me, though he may die, he shall live."*[31]

The grave will no longer hold the dead, and groaning will no longer hold the living.[32] The time for *"the redemption of our body"* will have come, and an instant change will take place. He *"will transform our lowly body that it may be conformed to His glorious body."*[33] Bodies that have known so many limitations, whether by illness, pain or deformity, will be instantly released. Minds that have been limited, from the most academic to the most seriously impaired, will be totally transformed. Physically and mentally, *"we shall be changed"*; and *"we shall be like Him"*[34] in answering glory. Like the redeeming work done firstly in our souls: physically, our new bodies will be perfected; and mentally, we shall know just as we also have been known.[35] We will be both transformed and conformed: changed from what we were like, and changed into what He is like. Oh, yes! We will resemble Him then, and no longer be concerned with differences, which, though important now, will no longer be applicable or matter.

A glorious throne

One of Paul's great lines of reasoning in his letter to the Romans describes believers as being like vessels in the hand of a potter. How apt this analogy is! Should my puny mind with its tinier thoughts challenge the infinite mind and eternal thoughts of God? He is the Potter. We are the clay, and our only thought should be to yield to His sovereign sway. We are His children to whom He is making known *"the riches of His glory on vessels of mercy, which He had prepared beforehand for glory."*[36] During our spiritual journey, like Jeremiah, we know that *"A glorious throne set on high from the beginning is the place of our sanctuary."*[37]

At every stage of that journey, we have access to its refuge as a place of asylum. It is high, from the beginning, and holy, because God is, and often we have unburdened ourselves and communed with Him there through the glorious name of the Man who intercedes for us. But soon the journey will be ended. This Man is coming out for us, and we are going in with Him to stand at the throne of His glory.

Isaiah prophesied of another day when *"there shall be a Root of Jesse, who shall stand as a banner to the people; for the Gentiles shall seek Him, and his resting place shall be glorious."*[38] In the following verses, he also prophesies that the Lord will *"recover the remnant of His people who are left"* and will *"assemble the outcasts of Israel."* This will happen, too, through the very same Man who will draw them by the very same means when he makes Himself known as the Man and Messiah of Calvary. Isaiah looked forward to this day and asks, *"Shall the earth be made to give birth in one day? Or shall a nation be born at once?"*[39] Yes, He will come to fulfil His purpose and promises for them, too.

Their day is coming but, before the dawning of that millennial day, and before the dark days prior to it, He will come for His church. We are going home as a glorious church, through His calling in the glorious gospel, and by His glorious appearing, to be with our Bridegroom at His glorious throne, and in this assurance we also know that *"His resting place shall be glorious."*

THE THINGS THAT ARE MADE
For since the creation of the world
His invisible attributes are clearly seen,
being understood by the things that are made,
even His eternal power and Godhead.
Will the thing formed say to him who formed it,
"Why have you made me like this?"
(Rom.1:20; 9:20)

If what is made were equal to its Maker,
Designer and designed would be as one:
Supreme would lose uniqueness and its power,
And Sovereignty would have its sway undone.

Creation would be great, yet in its splendour,
Would make the Former equal to the formed,
And glory that excludes there is One greater
Concludes that such a Glory must be spurned.

If finite has no Infinite behind it,
And creature and Creator are as one,
This also means the creature's own Creator
Is a created Being – creation,

Instead of all-creating and upholding –
Instead of the eternal God He is:
And man creates a god of his own making,
Instead of recognising Him and His.

For what is made can never match its Maker:
He stands Supreme, Designer, Sovereign God,
And subject to His glory as Creator
Helps us submit to own Him as our Lord.

Our finite bows at the Infinite's pleasure,
Upheld and re-created, by Him made;
And, growing in His grace and in His image,
His power, unique, eternal is displayed.

11

THE BRIDE, THE WIFE OF THE LAMB

"Now I saw a new heaven and a new earth, for the first heaven and the first earth had passed away. Also there was no more sea. Then I, John, saw the holy city, New Jerusalem, coming down out of heaven from God, prepared as a bride adorned for her husband. And I heard a loud voice from heaven saying, "Behold, the tabernacle of God is with men, and He will dwell with them, and they shall be His people. God Himself will be with them and be their God. Then one of the seven angels who had the seven bowls filled with the seven last plagues came to me and talked with me, saying, "Come, I will show you the bride, the Lamb's wife." And he carried me away in the Spirit to a great and high mountain, and showed me the great city, the holy Jerusalem, descending out of heaven from God" (Rev.21:1-3,9,10).

Two essential statements come together in these verses, as they do throughout the Revelation: *"I saw"* and *"he showed,"* and these include events from the present stage of the church and the churches, the end times, and the eternal state:

- The Revelation itself (1:1);
- Things which must take place after the church period (4:1);
- The judgment of Babylon, the mother of harlots (17:1);
- The bride, the Lamb's wife (21:9);
- The great city, the holy Jerusalem (21:10);
- A pure river of water of life (22:1);
- The confirmation and conclusion of the Revelation (22:6).

Right from the opening sentences of chapter 1, John was commended as one *"who bore witness to the word of God, and to the testimony of Jesus Christ, to all things that he saw."* His faithfulness in speaking about things he saw in heaven was consistent with what he saw on earth. Before closing his gospel record, he confirmed that *"he who has seen has testified, and his testimony is true."*[1] What a joy it must have been to him that what he was shown in Revelation 21 is the outcome of what he saw at the cross!

Eternity

By looking into Revelation 21, we are privileged to look into eternity to see the eternal glory of Christ and to anticipate being there with Him. In the ultimate triumph of His purpose the One who declares in verse 5, *"Behold, I make all things new"* (from *kainos*, meaning new in kind) will prove it to be true. By means of His new (*kainos*) covenant, He will bring His bride, who is made up of the *"new [kainos] creation"*[2] of all believers in Christ, into the New (*kainos*) Jerusalem surrounded by a new (*kainos*) heaven and new (*kainos*) earth. Everything is new and no part of it is the old refurbished. The Builder is with His church, the Head is with His body, and the Bridegroom is with His bride in the holy city, the New Jerusalem. It is the complete fulfilment of Genesis 2 where Eve was made all three to Adam. Revelation 21 also includes gold and precious stones[3], a river and the tree[4], which remind us of the Garden of God in Genesis 2 – the tree in v.9, the river in v.10, and gold and precious stones in vv.11 and 12. What a beautiful link there is between the Garden of God and the future City of God!

Some think that the holy city is the bride of Christ, but John says he saw it *"coming down out of heaven from God prepared* [Gr. *hetoimazō*] *as a bride for her husband."* It bears bridal character, as the place Jesus had in mind when He said, *"I go to prepare [hetoimazō] a place for you"*[5]: a prepared place, which is different from the bride who prepared [*hetoimazō*] herself in chapter 19:7. It's also the place that Abraham saw when *"he looked forward to the city which has foundations, whose builder and maker is God."*[6] Others also died in faith, having embraced, as if with open arms, what they didn't live to see. Even so, they longed for something better to be revealed in a heavenly place, *"Therefore God is not ashamed to be called their God, for He has prepared* [from Gr. *hetoimazō*] *a city for them."*[7]

Two other features also are worth considering: *"the wall of the city had twelve foundations, and on them were the names of the twelve apostles of the Lamb."*[8] This is their everlasting identity with the New Covenant and their relationship with the church, which is His body. We know that the city will have a *"high wall with twelve gates, and twelve angels at the gates, and names written on them, which are the names of the twelve tribes of the children of Israel."*[9] We also know that the cross work of our Lord Jesus Christ covers all who died in faith in Old Testament days, and that it will bring a future remnant into New covenant blessing.[10] These Scriptures join in confirming that all those redeemed ones dwell in *"the great city, the holy Jerusalem."*

In keeping with the new heaven and new earth, the city also is new, which means they are new in state and kind. The city also is described as holy, and this leads us to interpret the symbolism of its cubic dimensions. The most holy place in the tabernacle was a cube, as it also was in the temple, and these help us to think of the New Jerusalem as a most holy place. Instead of the ark of the covenant residing and the cloud presiding, *"the Lord God Almighty and the Lamb are its temple."* They are its ever-present glory.

History and Prophecy

History speaks very graphically of powerful kings and their kingdoms. For instance, the revelation given by God through Daniel was of an enormous image that depicted successive world powers, which came for a time and then were defeated. Starting at the top, it had a head of gold that was replaced by a chest and arms of silver, then by a belly and thighs of brass, legs of iron, and feet of iron and clay. It's a picture of the diminishing glory of kingdoms represented by gold, silver, copper, iron and clay. They also grew more splintered: the first had one head; the second had two arms; the third for the midriff also had four heads;[11] and the last had two legs of iron that end with ten toes of iron and clay.

Later, he portrayed one as a ram that *"did according to his will and became great"* (KJV) until it was confronted by a he-goat that snapped the ram's two horns. The he-goat *"grew very great, but when he became strong, the large horn was broken."*[12] The ultimate composition of iron and clay is an evident admixture resulting from an alliance made through the intermarriage of different peoples.[13]

This is where history becomes prophecy for, significantly, it's not another world power in the guise of another fierce animal that causes the whole image to tumble. It's *"a stone"*![14] By toppling the image, all four kingdoms, whether of gold or silver or brass or iron in their fading glory, will be destroyed by a single blow. Not only are they broken, they will be *"crushed together, and become like chaff from the summer threshing floors; the wind carried them away so that no trace of them was found."*

What sort of *"stone"* will do this? First of all, it's a *"stone that was cut out of the mountain without hands."* It is not of human origin, but is the One who said to His Father, *"A body You have prepared for Me."*[15] He is *"The stone which the builders rejected"*[16] and the One who said of His divine power, *"And whoever falls on this stone will be broken; but on whomever it falls, it will grind Him to powder."*[17] Some interpret this as comparing one degree of judgment with another, but the Lord may have been using it to show the contrast between those who fall on Him in repentance and brokenness and those on whom He falls in condemnation. This is the *"stone"* who will overcome and, when He does, an announcement will be made in heaven: *"The kingdom of this world has become the kingdom of our Lord and of His Christ, and He shall reign forever and ever."*[18] With unsurprising humility, He is seen as the understated *"stone,"* just as we also read of Him as a worm, a Lamb, a hen, as bread, and as a servant. Even so, we know that the worm defeated the serpent, the Lamb overcame the lion, the hen withstood the fox, the bread sustains all who believe, and we own the Servant as our Master and Lord.

World powers conquer until they are conquered. Their rule ends, their reigns finish, and their apparent power is shown to be clothed in weakness. They were potent, but not omnipotent! Unlike earthly kings, including Nebuchadnezzar whom the Lord GOD called *"king of kings,"*[19] the One who alone is King of kings will reign forever and ever. His kingdom will have no end, His power will never finish, and His apparent weakness is clothed in power! It's also not surprising that He doesn't resort to animal-like imagery to confront earthly powers, but reserved His likeness to the ram and to the he-goat for a very different battle. In contrast, He came as the answer to another ram: the one that was caught by its horns in Genesis 22:13, to show that He became willingly defenceless as our Substitute on the cross. He also fulfilled the imagery of other he-goats: first of all, as our atoning sacrifice and sin-bearer foreshadowed in Leviticus 16, and as the he-goat that was both *"majestic in pace"* and *"stately in walk"* in Proverbs 30:29,31.

John's writings always bring the sovereignty of God in Christ to the forefront. The first chapter of his Gospel declares Him to be God and King, and his letters present Him as co-equal with God in life, light and love. There is never any doubt that the sovereignty of God is being shown on earth. The Revelation is no different, but now there is an added emphasis that His sovereignty is being seen in heaven. All the divine judgments being poured out on the earth will bring the terror of the false Christ – the antichrist, the man of sin, the beast – to an end, and both he and the false prophet will be cast into the lake of fire.[20]

Before this, heaven also will witness the fall of the false bride, *"Babylon the great, mother of harlots and of the abominations of the earth,"* and an angel will be sent down from heaven to proclaim, *"Fallen, fallen is Babylon the great!"*[21] She has been the home of all evil and corruption, politically, religiously, morally and economically; her power is demonic, and nations will be deceived by her *"sorcery."* This is the Greek word *pharmakeia* from which we get our word pharmacy. However, the real connotation here is much more sinister, and probably has more to do with trade in drugs with all the hallucinations attached to witchcraft. In her fall, everything comes to a standstill and the voice of Babylon's entertainment and trade is silenced. Like the nations described by Daniel, *"Babylon shall be thrown down and not be found anymore."* In summing up her desolation, the mighty angel announced, *"The light of a lamp shall not shine in you anymore, and the voice of bridegroom and bride shall not be heard in you anymore."*[22]

The marriage of the Lamb

Immediately, the tone changes and, in contrast to the absence of bridal joy on earth, there is an outburst of bridal celebration in heaven. A great multitude join in saying, *"Alleluia; Salvation and glory and honour, and power, unto the Lord our God!"* (KJV). This triumphant call will bring an instant response from the twenty-four elders and the four living creatures: *"Amen! Alleluia!"* It is then that a voice from the throne, possibly of the Lord Jesus Christ Himself, will make the great announcement that should thrill us as we read: *"Praise our God –* which implies on-going praise *– all you His servants and those who fear Him, both small and great!" And I heard, as it were, the voice of a great multitude, as the sound of many waters and as the sound of mighty thunderings, saying, "Alleluia! For the Lord God Omnipotent reigns! Let us be glad and rejoice and give Him glory, for the marriage of the Lamb has come, and His wife has made herself ready."*[23]

Suddenly, at the sound of the fourth "Alleluia!" heaven's focus is entirely directed to the Bridegroom and His bride. Having just witnessed divine sovereignty applied by force on earth, the scene is set for heaven to witness the outcome of the greatest act of divine sovereignty that ever was shown in love, as He gave Himself *"for me"* and *"for us"* and *"for her,"*[24] His church and bride. This will be the moment when *"the purpose of the ages"*[25] will see the plan of eternity past brought to glorious fulfilment in eternity to come in those whose names were written in the Book of Life from the foundation of the world.[26] It's also the moment that was foreshadowed as God brought Eve to Adam, as Rebekah was led to Isaac, and as Ruth was married to Boaz. Our last Adam, our Isaac – the Seed - and our Boaz – the Redeemer - has been waiting, and so has His bride.

It is very common in eastern custom for marriage celebrations to be spread over different days and, sometimes, locations. This would appear to be the scriptural sequence of our bridal relationship with the Saviour, and we can consider it in three parts:

*Betrothal

At the moment of our salvation, we also entered into a multi-faceted union with Him. For instance, we became sheep of His flock, members of His body, subjects of the King, and children of God. As far as timing is concerned, our relationship with the Saviour began when we responded to the call of God in the gospel. It was then that we personally entered into the security of His assurance: *"All that the Father gives Me will come to Me, and the one who comes to Me I will by no means cast out."*[27] This means that the work of Christ has brought us into an eternal future with Him, since being children of God makes us *"heirs of God and joint heirs with Christ."*[28]

Along with the work of Christ, the work of the Spirit also guarantees our eternal future with Christ. It's of this Paul wrote in Ephesians 1:13,14, *"In Him you also trusted, after you heard the word of truth, the gospel of your salvation; in whom also, having believed, you were sealed with the Holy Spirit of promise, who is the guarantee of our inheritance until the redemption of the purchased possession, to the praise of His glory."* As we already thought in Chapter 2, the Holy Spirit is our *arrhabōn*, the engagement ring of our forthcoming marriage and eternal inheritance with Christ when all the redeemed go home at His coming.

*The marriage

With no doubt whatsoever, we will stand at His side knowing that we have been fitted through the promise of the gospel that *"many will be made righteous."*[29] The work is all His! We have been redeemed by the blood of the Lamb, delivered from the wrath of the Lamb, our names are in the Book of Life of the Lamb, so we look forward to being united with him in the marriage of the Lamb and to be with Him at the marriage supper of the Lamb. The Revelation speaks of all five. In the greatest of all senses, He has made His bride ready, and we will never forget it.

The emphasis here, however, is, *"His wife has made herself ready."* The next verse adds, *"And to her it was granted to be arrayed in fine linen, clear and bright, for the fine linen is the righteous acts of the saints."*[30] What a choice thought, that the glory of the bride includes what we have done for Him! It means that bridal preparation is being made in the Christlikeness of individuals in every corner of the world. From Pentecost to the Rapture, the Lord has noted their righteous acts. Many have known the hardship of standing for Him in darkest centuries, others *"were counted worthy to suffer shame for His name"*[31] in the face of severe persecution.

To them, it also could be said, *"For to you it has been granted on behalf of Christ, not only to believe on Him, but also to suffer for His sake."*[32] The secret is, it was *"granted"* to them, and the word here – charizomai – implies given by grace. So, even though the deeds were theirs, the grace was His! Just as they were given grace to believe, they were given grace to suffer. Nevertheless, He takes account of it all, which reminds us that *"The eyes of the LORD are in every place."*[33] Saints in remotest villages of the world may feel they are unknown. Lonely brothers or sisters may faithfully sustain what they feel is an unseen work. But no one is overlooked by the One who views His bride as being *"arrayed"* in acts that were for Him, even though He enabled them! He not only regards them, He rewards, and many will discover this to their praise when He reviews our lives at His judgment seat.[34]

*The marriage supper

After announcing the marriage, a blessing is given to those who are invited to attend and share in *"the marriage supper of the Lamb."* Hebrews 11 shows that Old Testament believers will be there, such as Abel, Noah, Enoch, Job, and all who lived by faith like Abraham. The redeemed of Israel will be there, included in John the Baptist's relationship as *"the friend of the bridegroom."*[35] Those *"who have the victory over the beast"*[36] will be there; as will many from the judgment of the living nations.[37] What a scene, when Old and New Testament believers see the fulfilment of all that was prophesied from Eden, and the Man of Calvary, the Lamb, is back on earth to rejoice and reign with His bride!

It's the fourth *"Blessed"* of seven given in the Revelation, beginning in chapter 1 and ending with chapter 22. On every occasion, the word for *"Blessed"* is *makarios*, which assures spiritual happiness whenever such blessings are enjoyed. Also in each case, earth is the place where the blessing is experienced, and this indicates that, although the marriage takes place in heaven, the marriage supper will take place on earth at the beginning of His 1,000-year reign. We can list them, as follows:

1. Rev.1:3 - *"Blessed is he who reads and those who hear the words of this prophecy, and keep those things which are written; for the time is near..."*: **In Christian service;**
2. Rev.14:13 - *"Blessed are the dead who die in the Lord from now on"*: **Tribulation martyrs;**

3. Rev.16:15 - *"Blessed is he who watches, and keeps his garments ..."*: **Christ's return to earth;**
4. Rev.19:9 - *"Blessed are those who are called..."*: **Marriage of the Lamb;**
5. Rev.20:6 - *"Blessed and holy is he ..."*: **Avoiding the second death;**
6. Rev.22:7 - *"Blessed is he who keeps the words ..."*:**Heeding the Revelation;**
7. Rev.22:14 - *"Blessed are those who do His commandments..."*:**Eternal access.**

Thinking of what lies ahead for the Bridegroom and His bride in the eternal scene fills our hearts with anticipation of being able to say of Him, *"He is altogether lovely,"*[38] and that He will say of us, *"The King's daughter is all glorious within."*[39]

GLORY AND GOODNESS

"Show me now Your way, that I may know You
and that I may find grace in Your sight ...
Please, show me Your glory."
(Ex.33:13,18)

His glory is high as the towering mountain, (Matt.17:1,2)
So lofty and grand in the glow of the sun;
His goodness, however, flows on like a fountain (Ps.7:5,9)
That pours out, unceasing, once it has begun.
We capture a glimpse of His infinite glory, (2 Cor.3:7,18)
Yet little retain of its glow on our face;
We must then return to the source of His goodness (Ex.34:29,35)
To know the renewing of refining grace.
The goodness of glory, the glory of goodness,
Our risen Redeemer confirms to His own

Are opened up to us in the way of the cross,
With more to be gained in the way of the Throne.
It is there we will stand at His side, as in judgment
He brings earthly chaos to moments of calm; (Rev.19:1)
Then mid Alleluias that swell His enthronement (Rev.19:1,3,4,9)
We will join in marital bliss with the Lamb. (Rev.19:7)

12

FURTHER THOUGHTS ON "FOREVER"

"Worthy is the Lamb who was slain to receive power and riches and wisdom, and strength and honor and glory and blessing." And every creature which is in heaven and on the earth and under the earth and such as are in the sea, and all that are in them, I heard saying: "Blessing and honor and glory and power be to Him who sits on the throne, and to the Lamb, forever and ever!" Then the four living creatures said, "Amen!" And the twenty-four elders fell down and worshiped Him who lives forever and ever" (Rev.5:12-14).

Journeys often are made more spectacular by their viewpoints: places specially set aside where travellers can pause, sometimes to take in what lies behind, but more often to gasp at the sight and sounds of what lies before. Our walk has been no different. Well might we look back on fascinating details of women God brought to the forefront with this highest intent, not only that they would fill a place in history, but that they would fulfil a place in prophecy and in His purpose. As their stories unfold, and we gather the cumulative effect of them, there's no doubt we have a rear mirror view of the journey they were on. But it may be worth asking the question: did any of them catch a forward glimpse of what God was doing through them?

It's the kind of question that may be answered by asking more questions. For instance, did Eve's perfect mind ever prompt her to ask the perfect question regarding what God had in mind when He gave her in absolute perfection to a perfect man? Did Rebekah ever wonder at the sequence of being brought to Isaac after his father, Abraham, had been prepared to take his life on the altar at Moriah? As far as the Shulamite is concerned, did she ever see the fluctuations in her relationship with Solomon as a reflection of Israel's with God? And did it ever occur to Ruth that finding the grace she knew she needed, and through a redeemer at that, pointed forward to the graciousness of God that was beyond the Law for a stranger?

It may be speculative to ask such questions about Old Testament shadows, but much less so to ask some rear-view questions about New Testament Christians. What we have in the opening chapter of the Revelation is a masterstroke of divine inspiration. To get the attention of His people who belonged to the seven churches in Asia, God gave a most striking vision of His Son. It can be taken as the first viewpoint or, perhaps more applicably to those churches, an observation post. Based on the fact that He was both visible and audible, surely they would be affected by seeing Him, even before they should sense the impact of seeing Him seeing them! Would they? Would the God-honouring assemblies in Philadelphia and Smyrna take comfort and worship; and would all the others accept the challenge and weigh their condition? Listening to His reviews, while looking back at the glory of His appearing to John, ought to have made them turn to see the voice that spoke with them, since John had already told them that this was the effect it had on him.

We do well to take stock ourselves, by asking if the revelation of the magnificent Person in chapter 1 is enough to stir our affections and appreciation. If not, will we pause after what He says to each church and acknowledge which one most resembles our own? Will we then bow at those feet of burnished brass that walk in judgment among the lampstands, until a look from His penetrating and purifying eyes of fire burns in us to His glory?[1]

> How shall I meet my Saviour's eyes,
> That fire which proves and purifies:
> A searching, penetrating gaze
> That estimates my words and ways,
> Will they be worthy of His praise?
>
> How shall I stand before His throne,
> My eyes cast down before His own?
> Or shall it be with gold, not dross;
> With joy, not grief; with gain, not loss;
> I trace the triumph of His cross?

Not knowing how each church responded in Asia, we must answer these questions for ourselves, especially bearing in mind that the Walker in the midst still wants to see a proper response to saying to all His churches, *"You are body of Christ."*

After these things

Whatever their immediate reaction, solace, sorrow or self-satisfaction, they were left to ponder the Saviour's assessment, as John moved on to the second and forward-looking viewpoint. Suddenly, their thoughts were turned from things that were taking place to *"Things which must take place after this."*[2] From having Him brought to a standstill at Laodicea's closed door, their view is turned upward to *"a door standing open in heaven."* Now, the One who walked among the lampstands is standing *"in the midst of the throne"*[3] as the slain Lamb. No longer the willingly defenceless Lamb of Calvary, yet bearing its scars, the victorious Lamb is both omnipotent, depicted by seven horns, and omniscient, portrayed by seven eyes.

This must have greatly moved John's heart for He loved the Lamb on earth, all the way to the cross and afterwards. As one of the eleven, he stood *"gazing up into heaven,"*[4] as Jesus rose on His journey into His Father's presence. What an immense change, to see Him there! The fresh impetus for exiled John must have been enormous, but would the forward-looking viewpoint make the same impression on seven churches that had just heard the details of His inward look?

The same question could be applied to ourselves, couldn't it? Like theirs, our service stands between these two great viewpoints: intentionally to be affected by the One who walks among the lampstands and by the accompanying vision of the Lamb on the throne. While the church is shielded from all that happens on earth from the time it is taken home at the rapture until the Lord's triumph at Armageddon, it will rejoice in the third viewpoint that allowed John to see the fall of Babylon the Great and hear the loud praise that results in heaven. If we take all three viewpoints, our present response should be to take encouragement from hindsight in the first, foresight in the second, and now insight in the third. Revelation 19 treats us to the bride's grandest moment when all heaven is jubilant over the marriage of the Lamb, and the very sight and sounds recorded should have dismissed every dubious action from the hearts and minds of those whose service in the early churches was doubtful, to say the least.

Every child of God in the present-day should, likewise, think of the splendour that awaits us and be filled with joy and assurance. The thought of bringing us near to Him by His blood in Ephesians 2:13, and taking us Home with Him at His coming in 1 Corinthians 15:23, leads on to bridal union with Him as His wife in Revelation 19:7 – near, nearer, and nearest of all! As we thought in our previous chapter, heaven's rejoicing spills over on earth in the marriage supper, and it's there we will reign with Him and with the redeemed from all ages for a thousand years. Could anything be better? Yes, for the earthly glory of that reign will seamlessly blend with *"the eternal kingdom of our Lord and Savior Jesus Christ"*[5] in the new heaven and new earth. Paul says of it:

> *"Then comes the end, when He delivers the kingdom to God the Father, when He puts an end to all rule and all authority and power. For He must reign till He has put all enemies under His feet. The last enemy that will be destroyed is death. For "He has put all things under His feet." But when He says "all things are put under Him," it is evident that He who put all things under Him is excepted. Now when all things are made subject to Him, then the Son Himself will also be subject to Him who put all things under Him, that God may be all in all."*[6]

How different will that be? Well, the new heaven and new earth will be the perfect setting for perfect service, and the fourth viewpoint will be the last and we will look on that unchangeable scene –

Forever

As we turn our attention to this unending *"forever,"* perhaps we should ask another question. If all the attributes of God are one, and always seen in their entirety in Christ, can we also conclude that all the aspects of His name will always be seen in Him, and that they are inseparably associated with Him as the Bridegroom? For example, He is:

- The last Adam and the Seed foreshadowed in Genesis;
- The Mediator and High Priest portrayed in Exodus;
- The Sacrifice and Altar depicted in Leviticus;
- The One who is Wonderful, Counsellor, Mighty God, Everlasting
- Father, Prince of Peace spoken of through Isaiah.

One of the great prophecies of God's Word is that He is *"making known unto us the mystery of his will, according to his good pleasure which he purposed in him unto a dispensation of the fulness of the times, to sum up all things in Christ, the things in the heavens, and the things upon the earth; in him."*[7] The eternal day is coming when new heavens and a new earth will see the wonder of *"things in the heavens, and things upon the earth"* united *"not only in this world, but also in that which is to come."*[8]

What a triumphant scene it will be, when *"an innumerable company of angels,"*[9] will form such a vital part of the gathered hosts, as the heaven and new earth unite in one! They are the holy angels who did not fall when Satan fell and perhaps drew *"a third of the stars of heaven"*[10] with him. Alongside them will be another great host: the redeemed of Israel from Old Testament days and the redeemed remnant from the great tribulation.[11] God will fulfil this wonderful promise to His ancient people,

"And so all Israel will be saved, as it is written: "The Deliverer will come out of Zion, and He will turn away ungodliness from Jacob; for this is My covenant with them, when I take away their sins."[12]

As mentioned in our last chapter, they will be accompanied by those whom the Lord Jesus will separate as *"sheep from the goats"*[13] in the judgment of the living nations. As a glorious testimony to the fact that, *"As for God, His way is perfect"*[14] and that *"His work is perfect,"*[15] the redeemed from other ages will be assembled around the church, which is the body of Christ. Altogether, they will rejoice in His ultimate glory being fully shown in this crescendo of all that God has planned for Him. He is *"head **of** the body, the church,"*[16] but then He will be *"head over all things **to** the church."* We have *"tasted that the Lord is gracious,"*[17] and being assured that we *"have tasted the good word of God and the powers of the age to come,"*[18] we know that God *"in the ages to come [He will] show the exceeding riches of His grace in his kindness toward us in Christ."*[19]

As we think of our place among such an enormous host, we may wonder what sort of service God has planned for us in eternity. So little is divulged, that it may be more profitable to ask what we are told about what this sublime "forever" holds for His Son. Thankfully, the letter to the Hebrews gives valuable help by showing us how the word is applied to Him.

*God and King

Hebrews 1:8 is very interesting. Although God spoke to His Son, He did not address Him as Son. Nor did He welcome His Servant home by calling Him Jesus. Instead, the Father's words were, *"Your throne, O God, is forever and ever."* This statement tells us that, when Jesus ascended to heaven, God gave His ultimate approval to His Son as God and as King.

He had done this in an earthly sense in John 6:27, by confirming, *"God the Father has set His seal on Him."* This was the divine seal of affection, approval and authority on the One whom He had sent with *"the food that endures to eternal life."*

With regard to time and His earthly work finished on the cross, God added His seal, as it were, on what He is *"forever."* His deity and majesty are sealed for eternity, which guarantees that all the redeemed will own Him as God and King when He sits on *"the throne of God and of the Lamb".*[20] We will be His subjects and *"the children whom God has given"*[21] Him *"forever."* This also means that the redeemed will own Him as both in an eternal bond as servants and subjects. We will rejoice together in the splendour of His majesty and in *"the glorious majesty of His kingdom,"* and be able to say in unison, *"Your kingdom is an everlasting kingdom."*[22] Two verses later, in Revelation 22:3, God adds, *"and His servants shall serve Him."* The wording here is very meaningful. It doesn't use the word *diakonos* for the work of menial servants, nor does it refer to *hupēretēs* as the under-oarsman type of servant. Instead, God retains the word *doulos*, which describes the bond that was formed through the gospel when we were *"set free from sin"* and became *"slaves of God."*[23] Having been bought by the precious blood of Christ, as of a lamb, and *"His servants will serve Him"* as God, as King, and as the Lamb *"forever."*

*Priest and Priesthood

The phrase we have just been thinking about comes from the Greek, *douloi autou latreusousin autō*, and could be translated as His bondservants will worship Him. Did the seven churches take particular note of this? If not, they should have done when they heard the word "servants" being applied to them in verse 6, as it was in chapters 1:1 and 2:20. They had just heard that there will be bondservants on the new earth, and they ought to have been living as such on the present earth. We can only wonder if they stopped to ask themselves if they really were. Now we can begin to envisage a service of ministering Godward, and the letter to the Hebrews gives further help by assuring us, *"The forerunner has entered for us, even Jesus, having become a High Priest forever."*[24] This also shows that He has a priesthood *"forever."* The Scriptures are silent regarding the kind of spiritual service that will take place *"in the eternal kingdom of our Lord and Savior Jesus Christ."*[25]

However, Hebrews 12:22-24 speaks of a vast arena of heavenly observers who presently show a combined interest in the priestly service of worshippers on earth. We can only begin to anticipate that the present gathering, made up of the *"church of the firstborn"* and *"the spirits of just men made perfect,"* points forward to the greater gathering of redeemed that will worship on the new earth with the Lord serving as High Priest forever. From his lowly vantage point, "dwelling in tents with Isaac and Jacob, the heirs with him of the same promise;" Abraham waited with faith's long-expectant look *"for the city which has foundations, whose builder and maker is God."*[26] [Heb 11:9,10] Such was His clear view of future glory that he also anticipated the presence of the incarnate Lord on earth for, as Jesus said, *"Abraham rejoiced to see My day, and he saw it and was glad."*[27] [John 8:56] What farsighted conversations there must have been in these tents, as three generations thought about their final home in *"the city"*!

There they will be with all those who *"died in faith,"* as Hebrews 11:13 tells us. They never received the promises, *"but having seen them from afar off were assured of them, embraced them and confessed that they were strangers and pilgrims on the earth."* In such a wonderful way they exhibited their expectation, not of a motherland, but, as the Greek word *patrida* in verse 16 implies, of their fatherland. The writer to Hebrews then adds this vital comment: *"Therefore God is not ashamed to be called their God, for He has prepared a city for them."* It's for the bride, for all the redeemed of Israel, and *"for them."* What a well-populated place of the redeemed of all time! The bride will rejoice with her Bridegroom and be surrounded by the most glorious unity that owns Him as their Redeemer, and be as one to own Him as Saviour, Shepherd, King and High Priest. It will be place of spiritual service, untainted holiness, unlimited in new bodies, and unconfined by eternity.

Around four thousand years after Abraham, God's promise is the mainstay of the Christian's expectation and, through it, we *"look for new heavens and a new earth in which righteousness dwells."*[28] [2 Pet 3:13] A sin-free world lies ahead, in which the Lord will prove in a new and far greater way than He promised through Hosea, "I will answer the heavens, and they shall answer the earth."[29] [Hos 2:21], and the blessings known, even in millennial fulness, will be eternally surpassed. Perhaps, we should encourage one another to follow Abraham's example by living in the assurance of what God has promised, to embrace it with all our hearts, and to live as strangers and pilgrims who are looking toward the homeland.

> Where no shade nor stain can enter,
> Nor the gold be dim,
> In His holiness unsullied,
> I shall walk with Him.
> Meet companion then for Jesus,
> From Him, for Him, made—
> Glory of God's grace forever
> There in me displayed.
> (Mrs. Bevan)

As John looked at the holy city, New Jerusalem, he noted something very different: *"I saw no temple in it, for the Lord God Almighty and the Lamb are its temple."*[30] It is a picture of the Father's eternal delight in His Son, that the words *naos autēs estin* really mean "is its temple." All three words are singular, to show Their on-going One-ness, and worshippers no longer focus on a dwelling place, but on a dwelling Person. It's as if God is able to look at the bride and say, "You are body of Christ," and look at the massed gathering of the redeemed and say, "You are temple of God."

Every blood-bought child of God rests on this, *"one sacrifice for sins forever ... has perfected forever those who are being sanctified."*[31] The perfecting of Old Testament believers also rests on what He has done for us, since *"they should not be made perfect apart from us."*[32] The same will apply to those who are redeemed during the great tribulation for they will overcome Satan *"by the blood of the Lamb"*[33] and be brought in to share in the forever-ness of what Christ has done.

*Saviour and Manhood

In his own wonderful way, the writer of Hebrews began by showing the Son as the eternal God and now ends by presenting Him as the eternal Man. Having served Him by faith in this world, we will serve Him by sight in the next. We will have changed at His coming to the air,[34] but *"Jesus Christ is the same yesterday, today, and forever."*[35] Hebrews also tells us *"He always lives,"*[36] and we know from verse 16 that He does so, *"according to the power of an endless life."* Because of this, *"The life that He lives, He lives to God,"* and we are *"alive to God in Christ Jesus."*[37] When Jesus said, *"Because I live, you will live also,"*[38] He gave us greater cause than John the Baptist to say that each of us *"rejoices greatly because of the Bridegroom's voice."*[39] He identified with our weakness, and we are identified with His might!

While there is much we do not yet know about our future service, we can be sure it will be eternally centred on One who as God, is King, High Priest, and great Shepherd. And in the midst of this vast amalgamated throng that rejoices in the united "forever" triumph of the everlasting covenant, He will be Bridegroom with His bride. In the only place where service can be all of these at once, we will see that His attributes are perfectly at one, and that all His names are too!

SEEING HIM – SEEING YOU
See the formerly Unseen
God in human form appears; (1 Tim.3:16)
Mark th'unmeasured gulf between
Everlasting – days and years. (Mic.5:2)
Time the Timeless drawing nigh,
As His mother birth awaits;
View the One who, from on high,
Lives by seasons, feasts, and dates. (Jn 5:1,2; 19:14)

On the circle of His heaven (Job 22:14)
Walking in His cloud-veiled state;
On the circle of the earth (Is.40:22)
Sits on His majestic seat.
See Him then descend to share,
Walking wearily to tell, (Jn 4:5,6)
And the great I AM declare, (Jn 4:26)
Seated there at Sychar's well.

Lowliness bows lower still,
Onward stooping to His cross; (Phil.2:8)

Then the Lamb on Calv'ry's hill
Bowed His lowest there for us.
Greater work was never done;
Deeper death was never died;
Heaven's love the battle won;
Hatred's hate then pierced His side. (Jn 19:34)

Hades at His voice was stirred (1 Pet.3:19)
By His proclamation there;
Death of death, yet Life of life,
Made His declaration where
Sinners bound within their prison
Never heard what we now hear:
Jesus lives, and He is risen! (1 Pet.3:22)
And His bride will soon be there!

13

CONCLUSION: OF HIM AND FOR HIM

"But of him are ye in Christ Jesus, who was made unto us wisdom from God, and righteousness, and sanctification, and redemption." *"All things were created through Him and for Him"* (1 Cor.1:30 RV; Col.1:16).

At the end of our journey, we can look backward and forward, and, by taking in all that is ours through saving grace, be caused to say, *"This was the Lord's doing, and it is marvellous in our eyes."*[1] We wouldn't hesitate to confess it is all *of Him*, nor would we fail to acknowledge that it is all *for Him*. Paul captured this in Colossians 1:16 when he wrote, *"All things were created through Him and **for Him**,"* and we gladly grasp this vital truth. They were made through the greatness of His power, and were made for the greatness of His glory. David said this in Psalm 19:1: *"The heavens declare the glory of God; and the firmament shows His handiwork,"* and readily agreeing we would add, so also did Eve. She was made both through Him and for Him. We can't fail to notice in the first of all the women God moved, that He declared His handiwork by making her and His glory by bringing her to her bridegroom. Little did she know that she was the perfect foreshadowing of the bride that God would make and bring to His Son.

We may not tend to think that sending Him for us was a creative act of God, but it was. 1 Corinthians 1:30 (RV) makes this very clear by telling us, *"But of him are ye in Christ Jesus, who **was made** unto us wisdom from God, and righteousness, and sanctification, and redemption."* Preparing a body for Him was a creative act, and so was making His attributes available to those who are a new creation.[2] Paul expands on this in the first eleven chapters of Romans where he presents the glory of the gospel through which *"many will **be made** righteous."*[3]

His lengthy presentation shows how costly a recreating work it took to change us from what we were in our sinful nature to what we are in Christ. As he traces the grace of God in our salvation, redemption, justification and glorification, he lifts our minds to think of the great thoughts that were in the mind of God. He gives a much abbreviated summary in 1 Corinthians 2:7 where he refers to *"the hidden wisdom which God ordained before the ages for our glory."* Before He had created anything, the desire to save sinners was in the heart of God, and this is what led Paul in Romans to sum up his eleven chapters by leading us to worship in the final verse: *"For **of Him** and **through Him** and to Him are all things, **to whom** be glory forever. Amen."*

We have been called by the God of glory and saved for the God of glory. In the same way, we belong to One who is the Rock, the Head and the Bridegroom. We are His building, His body, and His bride. He is the Workman; we are His workmanship. He is exalted in glory; we are humbled in worship and willingly say, *"through Jesus Christ, to whom be glory forever and ever. Amen."*[4]

CONCLUSION: OF HIM AND FOR HIM

THE REST OF THE WAY

O fathomless mercy, O infinite grace,
In humble thanksgiving, the road I retrace;
Thou never hast failed me, my strength and my stay;
To whom should I turn for the rest of the way?

*

Through danger, through darkness, by day and by night
Thou ever hast guided and guided aright.
I have trusted in Thee and peacefully lay
My head in Thy hand for the rest of the way.

*

Thy cross all my refuge, Thy blood all my plea,
None other I need, blest Redeemer, but Thee.
I need not fear shadows that enshroud me today
For Thou wilt go with me the rest of the way.

(Laura Kern Sawyer)

FOOTNOTES

PREFACE

(1) Grace in First Peter, The Apostle Jude's Tripod, Boaz – Ruth's Bridegroom, Redeemer and Lord of the Harvest. All three books published by Hayes Press in 2019 (2) Rev.21:9 (3) Lk.24:15 (4) Lk.24:27 (5) Lk.24:32

1. THINGS CONCERNING HIMSELF

(1) 2 Cor.10:1 (2) Is.53:2 (3) Zech.9:9 (4) Matt.11:29 (5) 1 Pet.1:11 (6) Heb.1:3 (7) Eph.1:21; 4:10 (8) Heb.1:8 (9) Eph.1:22; 5:23 (10) Is.53:7 (11) 1 Cor.1:25 (12) 1 Jn 3:12 (13) Acts 3:14 (14) 2 Cor.13:4 (15) Jn 18:6 RV (16) Rom.6:9 (17) Is.53:3 ESV (18) Eph.1:6; 5:25 (19) Is.53:12 (20) Col.2:14 ESV (21) Eph.5:25 (22) 1 Thess.4:14-17

2. A BRIDE THROUGH BLOOD

(1) Gen.3:13; 2 Cor.11:3; 1 Tim.2:14 (2) Ezek.31:8,9 (3) Gen.1:26 (4) 1 Cor.15:45 – quoted from Gen.2:7 (5) Gen.2:18 (6) Eccl.3:11 (7) 1 Cor.15:49 KJV (8) Rev.19:6-9 (9) Eph.1:4 (10) Rev.13:8 (11) 1 Cor.15:22 (12) Matt.16:18 (13) Jn 6:37 (14) Jn 6:37-44 (15) Rom.16:25 (16) Col.1:26 (17) Matt.11:27 (18) Eph.4:16 (19) 1 Cor.12:6 (20) Eph.3:10,11 (21) Eph.5:24 (22) Eph.1:22,23 (23) Gal.2:20 (24) 1 Cor.6:20 (25) Jn 13:10; 15:3 (26) Jn

3:5 (27) Jn 3:11 (28) Jas.1:18 – see also 1 Thess.2:13; 1 Pet.1:23 (29) Jas.1:21 (30) 2 Thess.2:13 RV (31) Col.1:22 (32) Heb.2:18 (33) Heb.13:5

3. A BRIDE THROUGH THE SPIRIT

(1) 2 Chron.3:1 (2) Jn 6:37; 12:32 (3) Gal.3:2 (4) Judg.11:35 RV (5) Heb.11:8 (6) Rom.4:11 (7) Mk.15:32 (8) Heb.11:1 (9) Gal.3:2 (10) 2 Cor.5:7 (11) Jn.16:14 (12) Eph.1:14 (13) 1 Pet.1:8 (14) Gen.24:28 (15) Gal.3:3 (16) Rom.8:14 (17) S of S 1:4 RV (18) Gen.24:36 (19) Job 42:5 (20) Job 19:27 (21) Tit.2:13 (22) Rev.22:20 ESV (23) Jn 14:2 (24) 2 Cor.5:6-8 (25) Eph.1:3

4. ISRAEL: A BRIDE FOR GOD

(1) Rom.3:20 (2) Rom.3:21 (3) Rom.4:5; 5:19 (4) 2 Pet.1:4 (5) Rom.7:12,14 RV (6) Heb.7:22 (7) Lev.26:3 (8) Rom.6:17 RV (9) Ps.37:1 (10) Ps.94:20 (11) Acts 8:23 RV (12) Ex.31:18 (13) 1 Chron.15:25 (14) 1 Chron.16:37-40 (15) 1 Kin.18:36 (16) 2 Kin.3:20 (17) Rom.15:4 (18) Jn 1:14, Young's Literal Translation (19) Heb.9:14 (20) Ex.25:22 (21) 1 Cor.15:43 (22) Gal.6:14 (23) Hos.2:16 (24) Is.54:5; 62:5 (25) Jer.2:2 (26) Ex 24:7 (27) Ezek. 16:8-12 (28) Gen 24:22, 53 (29) Ruth 3:3 (30) Tit.3:5 (31) 2 Cor.1:21; 1 Jn 2:20, 27 (32) 2 Cor.5:1-5; Tit.2:10 (33) Heb.10:25 (34) 2 Tim.4:2 (35) Acts 10:42

5. THE SHULAMITE: A BRIDE FOR THE KING

(1) Song 1:1 (2) Song 6:13 (3) Rom.7:18 (4) Gal.2:20 (5) Eph.1:6 (6) Rom.5:2 (7) Eph.5:27 (8) Song 7:1 (9) Rom.10:15 (10) Rev.2:4 (11) Ps.104:33,34 KJV (12) Heb.10:19-25 (13) 1 Cor.10:21 (14) Ps.118:12 (15) Ps.69:2 (16) 1 Pet.2:24 (17) Ex.15:23; Ruth 1:20 (18) Mk.14:3 (19) Phil.3:10 (20) 1 Sam.25:29 (21) Is.5:1-4 (22) Song 6:13; 7:11,12 (23) Rom.14:17 (24) Jn 6:37 (25) 2 Pet.1:19 (26) 1 Cor.1:6,8 (27) Matt.2:11; Mk.15:23; Jn 19:39 (28) Lev.2:1,2; Eph.5:2 (29) Heb.12:2; Is.53:11 (30) Eph.5:2 (31) Song 5:4

RV (32) Song 1:14

6. RUTH: A BRIDE THROUGH REDEMPTION

(1) Is.28:21 KJV (2) Josh.24:2 (3) Gen.31:30 (4) Ex.12:12 (5) Gen.19:36,37 (6) e.g. Judg.3:14,20,21 (7) Num.21:29 (8) Matt.1:5 (9) Ruth 1:8 (10) 1 Sam.22:3 (11) Ruth 1:16-18 (12) Jn 15:14 (13) Rev.1:9 (14) Eph.4:25 (15) Ruth 2:2,13, Young's Literal Translation (16) Matt.9:38 (17) Eph.1:3 (18) Eph.2:6,10; 6:11-14 (19) Ps.110:1 (20) Eph.2:6 (21) Lev.26:12 (22) 2 Cor.6:16 (23) Ex.33:21 (24) Amos 9:1 (25) Rom.5:2 (26) Rom.9:11 (27) Ps.17:8 (28) Jn 6:35 (29) 1 Cor.12:13 NASB (30) Is.12:3 (31) v.14; Ruth 2:14 (32) Ruth 2:7 (33) 1 Jn 1:3 (34) 2 Sam.22:31 (35) Heb.12:2

7. A BRIDAL RESEMBLANCE IN THE CHURCHES

(1) Rev.21:1 (2) 1 Sam.25:3 (3) Eph.1:22,23 (4) Eph.1:22,23 (5) Matt.16:18 (6) Rom.8:29 (7) Rom.1:9 (8) 1 Cor.1:9 (9) Gal.4:6 (10) Job 42:3 (11) 1 Pet.1:3 (12) Matt.16:18 (13) 1 Pet.2:4 (14) Matt.11:28 (15) Heb.4:16; 7:25; 10:22 (16) 1 Pet.2:5 (17) Rom.16:25 (18) Eph.4:12,13 (19) 1 Cor.12:18 (20) 2 Cor.4:14 (21) Col.1:28 (22) 2 Cor.3:17 (23) Jn 6:39,40

8. SEEING THE DIFFERENCES

(1) Phil.1:10 (2) Col.1:15 (3) Jn 15:22 (4) 1 Cor.12:13 (5) 1 Tim.4:15 (6) Jn 15:5 (7) Col.2:19 (8) Jn 3:30 (9) Matt.11:29 RV (10) Matt.28:19,20 (11) Acts 14:21,22 (12) 1 Cor.4:1,2 (13) 2 Tim.4:20

9. SUFFERING OR REJOICING

(1) 1 Cor.12:13 RV (2) Jn 1:33 (3) 1 Cor.11:18 (4) Acts 2:42 (5) Acts 2:44 (6) Is.63:9 (7) Jn 11:35 (8) Lk.7:13 (9) Ps.54:4 RV (10) 1 Cor.12:18 (11) Col.4:17 (12) 1 Tim.4:14 (13) 1 Cor.12:27 (14) Phil.3:14 RV (15) 2 Tim.1:9 (16) Heb.3:1 (17) 2 Cor.5:9 (18) Gen.2:24; Matt.19:5,6 (19) Eph.5:30 (20) Eph.3:9 (21) Mk.8:38; 13:27; 1 Tim.5:21 (22) Matt.25:41 (23) 1 Pet.1:12 (24) Heb.2:14

10. A GLORIOUS CHURCH

(1) Jude 24 (2) Job 38:7 (3) Lk.2:10-14 (4) Lk.15:10 (5) Jude 6 (6) 2 Pet.2:4 (7) Ps.29:3; Acts 7:2 (8) Eph.1:17-23 (9) 1 Cor.2:8; Jas.2:1 (10) Rom.4:25 (11) Jn 16:8; 2 Thess.2:13; 1 Pet.4:14 (12) Rom.8:21 (13) Ps.19:1 (14) Ex.15:1 (15) Ex.3:13,14 (16) Is.52:6 (17) Col.1:11 (18) Tit.3:5 (19) Jer.50:34 (20) Is.63:12 (21) Is.53:1 (22) Is.30:30 (23) Ps.60:6 (24) 1 Tim.1:11 (25) Titus 2:13 (26) 2 Tim.1:10 (27) Tit.2:13,14 (28) 1 Thess.4:16,17 (29) Lk.13:17 (30) 1 Cor.15:52,53 (31) Jn 11:25 (32) Rom.8:23 (33) Phil.3:21 (34) 1 Jn 3:2 (35) 1 Cor.13:12 ESV (36) Rom.9:20-23 (37) Jer.17:12 ESV (38) Is.11:10 (39) Is.66:8

11. THE BRIDE, THE WIFE OF THE LAMB

(1) Jn 19:35 (2) 2 Cor.5:17 (3) Rev.21:11,18,19 (4) Rev.22:2 (5) Jn 14:2 (6) Heb.11:10 RSV (7) Heb.11:10,16 (8) Rev.21:14 (9) Rev.21:12 (10) Jer.31:31; Heb.8:7-13 (11) Dan.7:6 (12) Dan.8:3-8 (13) Dan.2:43 (14) Dan.2:34 (15) Heb.10:5 (16) 1 Pet.2:7 (17) Matt.21:44 (18) Rev.11:15 ESV (19) Ezek.26:7 (20) Rev.19:20 (21) Rev.17:5; 18:2 ESV (22) Rev.18:21-24 (23) Rev.19:5-7 (24) Gal.2:20; Tit.2:14; Eph.5:25 (25) Eph.3:11 RVM (26) Rev.17:8 (27) Jn 6:37 (28) Rom.8:17 (29) Rom.5:19 (30) Rev.19:8 (31) Acts 5:41 (32) Phil.1:29 (33) Prov.15:3 (34) 1 Cor.3:12-14; 4:5; 2 Cor.5:10 (35) Jn 3:29 (36) Rev.15:2 (37) Matt.25:31-46 (38) Song 5:16 (39) Ps.45:13 NASB

12. FURTHER THOUGHTS ON "FOREVER"

(1) Rev.1:14,15 (2) Rev.4:1 (3) Rev.5:6 (4) Acts 1:11 (5) 2 Pet.1:11 ESV (6) 1 Cor.15:24-28 (7) Eph.1:9,10 RV (8) Eph.1:21 RV (9) Heb.12:22 (10) Lk.10:18; Rev.12:4 (11) Zech.14:2 (12) Rom.11:26,27 (13) Matt.25:32 (14) 2 Sam.22:31 (15) Deut.32:4 (16) Col.1:18 (17) 1 Pet.2:3 (18) Heb.6:5 (19) Eph.2:7 (20) Rev.22:1 (21) Heb.2:13 (22) Ps.145:5,12,13 (23) Rom.6:18,22 (24) Heb.6:20 (25) 2 Pet.1:11 ESV (26) Heb.11:9,10 (27) John 8:56 (28) 2 Pet.3:13 (29) Hos.2:21 (30) Rev.21:22 (31) Heb.10:12,14 (32) Heb.11:40 (33) Rev.12:11 (34) 1 Cor.15:51,52 (35) Heb.13:8 (36) Heb.7:25 (37) Rom.6:10,11 (38) Jn 14:19 (39) Jn 3:29

13. CONCLUSION

(1) Mk.12:11 (2) 2 Cor.5:17 (3) Rom.5:19 (4) Heb.13:21

ABOUT THE AUTHOR

Andy was born in Glasgow, Scotland, He came to know the Lord in 1954, and was baptized in 1958. He is married to Anna, and he lives in Kilmacolm, Scotland. They have two daughters and one son. He entered into full-time service in 1976 with the churches of God (www.churchesofgod.info). He has engaged in an itinerant ministry in western countries and has been privileged to serve the Lord in India and Myanmar (formerly Burma).

MORE BOOKS FROM ANDY MCILREE

Grace in First Peter - The Many-Splendoured Grace Shown to an Ungracious Man (Men God Moved - Book One)

As Andy says, "Tracing the grace of God in Peter's first letter is like seeing the glory of God in Romans and the greatness of God in Hebrews." In this deeply practical book, Andy takes us through each of Peter the rough fisherman's 5 chapters, and introduces us to the manifold grace of God expressed in at least 11 different aspects:

1. GRACE REQUIRED IN AN UNGRACIOUS MAN
2. GRACE RESTORED IN OUR MISTAKES
3. GRACE RECEIVED IN THE GOSPEL
4. GRACE REGARDED IN WORSHIP AND WITNESS
5. GRACE REINFORCED IN TRIALS
6. GRACE RECIPROCATED IN MARRIAGE
7. GRACE RECOGNISED IN HOLINESS
8. GRACE REVEALED IN SPIRITUAL GIFTS
9. GRACE REFLECTED IN LEADERSHIP
10. GRACE REGAINED IN BIBLICAL TRUTH
11. GRACE RE-EMPHASISED IN PAUL'S LETTERS

The Apostle Jude's Tripod - The Man, Method and Message of the New Testament's Forgotten Book (Men God Moved - Book Two)

The apostle Jude's little letter can easily be read within five minutes, yet it spans eternity past and future, history and prophecy, blessing and judgment, past revelation and fresh revelation, things known and not known, heaven's glory and hell's grief. And, like all Scripture, it has a God-given relevance for us in the present day:

* for reproof – showing when we are off track
* for correction – helping us to get back on track
* for instruction – enabling us to keep on track.

As Jude wrote his little book, it's as if he did so with the mindset of a surveyor, scanning the worrying spiritual landscape in front of him - 19 times in his short letter, Jude moves his surveyor's 'tripod' of threes to drive his point home. In addition to exploring each of these, Bible teacher Andy McIlree unpacks each verse across seven key themes of Salutation, Salvation, Contention, Condemnation, Revelation, Benediction and Doxology.

This is a very enlightening and practical study of a little understood, under-appreciated and often forgotten part of our New Testament.

Boaz: Ruth's Bridegroom, Redeemer, and Lord of the Harvest (Men God Moved - Book Three)

The events of the book of Ruth are like a jewelled cameo woven into the fabric of Israel's chequered background. The account of Ruth's arrival on the pages of God's Word is an interweaving of His grace, His call – so typical of His reaching out to Abraham, Rahab, and to Gentiles – and His purpose. So, during Israel's dull days, she is like a colourful butterfly emerging from a very drab chrysalis. There is no shallow end to the story of Ruth, as depths of despair at the beginning lead on to deepening delight, which causes us to exclaim, "Oh, the depth of the riches both of the wisdom and knowledge of God! How unsearchable are His judgments and His ways past finding out! Join Bible teacher Andy McIlree in this heart-warming study as, chapter by chapter, he explores the depths of this wonderful Old Testament book, and in particular how Boaz is a picture of the Lord Jesus as our kinsman-redeemer, bridegroom and the Lord of the harvest.

The Five Solas of the Reformation

Five centuries after Luther nailed his Ninety-five Theses to the door of a Catholic church, is there still a need for reformation? Yes, the Reformers' 'Five Solas' - Scripture Alone, Christ Alone, Grace Alone, Faith Alone, the Glory of God Alone - should be engraved on all our hearts, and the need could hardly be greater for them to be nailed to the doors of today's shallow churches today that are in danger of "being destroyed for lack of knowledge" (Hosea 4:6).

MORE BOOKS FROM ANDY MCILREE

Garments for Glory

This book is an indispensable in-depth study of the types and shadows (pictures) of Christ in Israel's High Priest under the Levitical Order of the Old Testament Tabernacle and Temple, and specifically how his work, person and clothing speak of Jesus as our Great High Priest on the throne of God. But this is far from a dry, scholarly endeavour; its meditations will make your heart soar in fresh appreciation of what God has so expertly revealed in His Word about His Son; and its challenges will help you consider afresh "how should we now live" in view of what God has revealed to us about His Son.

ABOUT THE PUBLISHER

Hayes Press (www.hayespress.org) is a registered charity in the United Kingdom, whose primary mission is to disseminate the Word of God, mainly through literature. It is one of the largest distributors of gospel tracts and leaflets in the United Kingdom, with over 100 titles and many thousands dispatched annually. In addition to paperbacks and eBooks, Hayes Press also publishes Plus Eagles' Wings, a fun and educational Bible magazine for children, and Golden Bells, a popular daily Bible reading calendar in wall or desk formats.

If you would like to contact Hayes Press, there are a number of ways you can do so:

By mail: c/o The Barn, Flaxlands, Royal Wootton Bassett, Wiltshire, UK SN4 8DY

By phone: 01793 850598

By eMail: info@hayespress.org

via Facebook: www.facebook.com/hayespress.org